KETTLEBELL SPORT

A TRAINING METHODOLOGY TUTORIAL BY DENIS VASILEV

SECOND EDITION

(REVISED AND UPDATED)

First Edition, 2015
ISBN: 979-8-9880288-1-9

Photograph credits:
Page vi: © Rik Fedyck Photo, Kettlebell Olsztyn
8, 74a: © Nazofoto
33a, 71, 82: © Rik Fedyck Photo
33b, 33c, 74b, 92: © Arejas Uzgiris
74c: © Matthew Belter

Other photographs courtesy of the author

Designed by Regine Sulit and Denis Vasilev
Edited by Ola Vasileva, Paolo Encarnacion, and Arejas Uzgiris

www.denisvasilevkettlebell.com

denisvasilevkettlebell.com

kettlebellworld.org

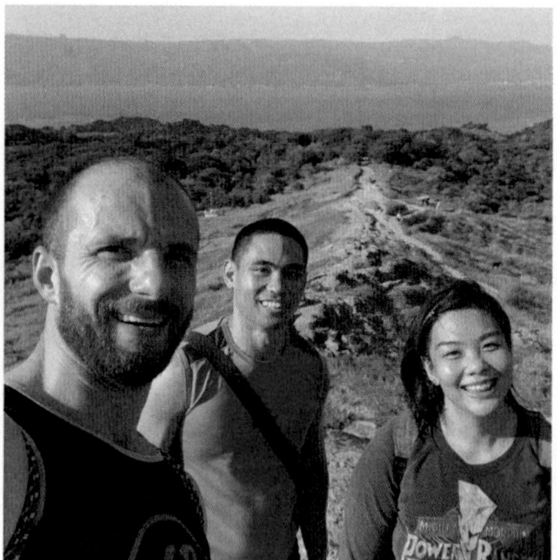

Grateful to my dear wife Ola and my dear friends Paolo and Regine.
I couldn't have done it without you.

The moment after a victory. IUKL European Championship 2012

My dear friend,

You have chosen a wonderful endeavor that is Kettlebell Sport.
This is a sport that will make you better in many ways.
It is a sport of patience and skill. It also requires a strong mind.
My sport motto is:
"Train as hard as you can and you'll love to compete.
Never quit and you'll respect yourself".

Good luck!
Denis Vasilev

Table of Contents

ABOUT THIS BOOK

The methodology I present in this book is the result of many years of work. It was first published in 2015 as part of my university thesis and only contained 47 pages. What you currently hold in your hands is the updated and expanded second edition. Where the first edition sought to present a general description of the most modern and effective training methods for kettlebell sport, this current edition now provides the specific details of each of these training methods. Each topic is described in depth with accompanying graphics and illustrations that are meant to serve as an additional learning aid.

Also included in this second edition are ready-to-implement beginner training programs for all three kettlebell sport exercises (Jerk, Snatch, and Long Cycle). I've also added advanced training program templates based on my most successful training cycles during my competitive career. Another significant addition is that I've divided this book into two main parts.

Part I tackles the nuts and bolts of programming, beginning with a brief history of how the modern training methods came to be. It also outlines the general training principles that underlie a rational kettlebell sport program. Afterwards, I discuss in-depth the actual methodology I use for constructing and arranging the different training elements. By the end of this section, you will be able to form a coherent and logical kettlebell sport program that you can use in your own training.

Part II contains an elaborate self-analysis of my own results during my career and is aimed to provide the reader with a general impression of how I applied my methodology to my own lifting. My hope is that my reflections can serve as a useful example of how you can analyze your own progress so that you can make better decisions that will improve your chances of success in kettlebell sport.

The intention of this book is to provide you with all the basic tools and foundational knowledge that will allow you to create a personalized and effective kettlebell sport program for yourself and for your students.

I'm certain that this will not be the last edition of my training methodology book. For now, I humbly present to you my most up-to-date collection and explanation of my training methods.

DEDICATION

> *"Even though I had a sense that I was already quite athletic growing up and being attracted to sports, I never considered myself an exceptionally outstanding athlete. I think my success is the result of performing consistent work, maintaining my passion to be good in what I do, having full faith in the people I work with, all the while relying on discipline and luck. I feel fortunate for all the serendipitous circumstances that came my way and how they played out."*

My life is intimately related to kettlebell sport. I started training in 1999, and on December 30 2004 I was awarded the rank of Master of Sport. Four years later, in 2008 I was able to achieve Master of Sport International Class but it was not until April 5 2010 that I would be officially awarded this rank. During my career, I was undefeated in professional competition from 2007 until my retirement from the Russian National Team in 2016.

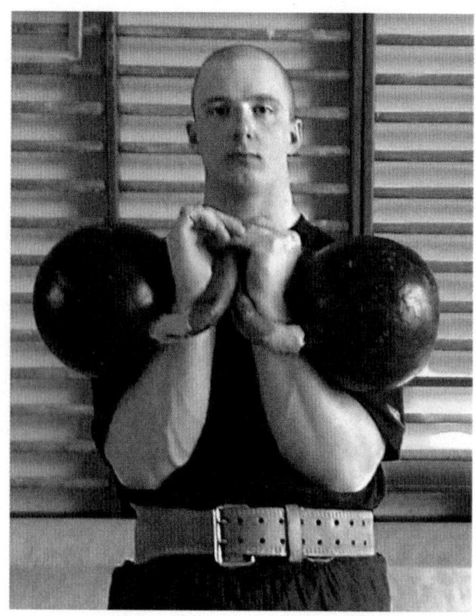
Denis Vasilev. Local competition 2004

Honestly, I'm still taken aback by the magnitude of all my achievements in kettlebell sport. Even though I had a sense that I was already quite athletic growing up and being attracted to sports, I never considered myself an exceptionally outstanding athlete. I think my success is the result of performing consistent work, maintaining my passion to be good in what I do, having full faith in the people I work with, all the while relying on discipline and luck. I feel fortunate for all the serendipitous circumstances that came my way and how they played out.

This has been a long and arduous yet rewarding journey for me. I would like to give thanks and recognition to the people, both known and unknown, who helped me each step of the way.

Under the guidance of my first martial arts coach Aleksandr Korovniy, I grew from an ordinary 7 year old boy into an athlete back in Kaliningrad, Russia. In 1998, at the age of 15, I already learned to love sports with all my heart. I understood then that I would never abandon it and that it would play a huge part in my life. Even after I chose to specialize in kettlebell sport, Aleksandr supported me and contributed a lot to my progress.

Denis Vasilev with Timofey Nikolaev

After transitioning to kettlebell sport, my physical culture school teacher and Master of Sport in Greco-Roman Wrestling Yuri Semizarov helped me reach Rank I in Biathlon with 24kg (70 repetitions in Jerk, 140 repetitions in Snatch, 140 points Biathlon total score). I was 17 years old and had only been training for less than two years.

My next achievement was to become a Candidate Master of Sport in Biathlon with 24kg (120 repetitions in Jerk, 160 repetitions in Snatch, 200 points Biathlon total score) under the guidance of Master of Sport in Gymnastics Gennadi Zelenin, who was also the kettlebell sport coach at the university I attended.

The defining moment that finally convinced me to pursue kettlebell sport as a career was when I witnessed firsthand multiple-time World Champion and Master of Sport International Class in Long Cycle Eduard Akhramenko lifting in competition. His personal record in Long Cycle was an unbelievable 95 repetitions and I consider him my first professional idol and inspiration in kettlebell sport. He was the first professional kettlebell lifter I saw in real life and seeing him drove me to seek out his coach, Timofey Nikolayev.

Timofey was a Master of Sport in Olympic Weightlifting and an Honored Coach of Russia. After seeing Eduard, I asked him to coach me. He agreed and we worked together from 2000 to 2005. I am grateful to him for making me a professional kettlebell lifter. Under his coaching and programming I achieved the rank of Master of Sport with 32kg in both Biathlon and Long Cycle in 2004 when I was 21 years old. Our results served as a solid foundation on which I would build on to reach my next goal of becoming Master of Sport International Class.

From 2005 to 2007, I took a break from kettlebell sport because I moved from Kaliningrad to Saint Petersburg. During this period I coached myself in bodybuilding and powerlifting. After my hiatus, it was Arkadi Semyonov who helped me regain my shape in kettlebell sport within just a few months. Under Arkadi's instruction, I was able to hit 83 repetitions in Long Cycle at the Championship of Saint Petersburg. This result allowed me to achieve my goal of becoming a Master of Sport International Class. More importantly, it would be enough to convince the legendary Sergey Rachinsky to become my coach.

Sergey and I were inseparable as coach and athlete from 2007 to 2017. He is an amazing expert in the art of mental preparation and his training methodology became the foundation on which I would later build on. It is no secret that I achieved my absolute best results under his coaching, beginning with our immediate victory during the 2008 European Championships. Despite all our victories, I consider hitting 100 repetitions with 2x32kg in Long Cycle our crowning achievement. This dream was realized in April 2015 in Vancouver, Canada. I was actually able to do 102 repetitions but the counter failed on the final repetition so my official result was 101 repetitions. This set is memorable to me and I can still feel the effortlessness of holding the perfect pace of 10 repetitions each minute. It was a flawlessly executed textbook set. I am extremely grateful to Sergey for all his amazing coaching and inspiration.

In 2009 I was already deeply interested in Sergey's methodology from a scientific point of view. Unfortunately, Sergey never wrote down any of our training plans on paper. All the information I received from him and all the tasks he gave me to accomplish were only given verbally. The only exceptions were when he was away and he wouldn't be able to tell me what to do in person. Incidentally, I started coaching other people around this time. It was out of this necessity that I began to gather and formalize Sergey's training principles and programming method.

Denis Vasilev with Arkadii Semenov (Switzerland, 2014)

The following year, in 2010, I became a student at the Lesgaft National State University of Physical Education, Sport and Health. Having won all the possible elite competitions multiple times by this point gave me a depth of practical experience that would serve me well as I worked in the Theory of Athleticism and Methodology department. I owe my success as a student to Gennady Vinogradov, Master of Sport in Olympic Weightlifting as well as chief and professor of the Theory of Athleticism and Methodology department, for his masterful leadership and scientific inspiration.

I am also grateful to Sergey Rudnev for accepting me as his student from January 2011 to June 2011. Under his coaching I won the 2011 IUKL European Championship and the 2011 Championship of Russia. It was an amazing experience and the insights I gained from his revolutionary method of incorporating 2kg increments with kettlebell training weights continue to benefit me to this day.

Being able to communicate and share my experiences with great athletes such as Sergei Merkulin, Igor Vitalyevich Novikov, Johnny Benidze, Andrei Kravtsov, Aleksandr Khvostov, and Ivan Denisov has also made a significant impact on my development as an athlete and coach. The ideas and methods contained in this book are much richer thanks to our shared correspondence and feedback.

Denis Vasilev with Sergey Rachinsky, 2008 Cup of Russia (left); 2008 IUKL European Championship, first MSIC victory. (right)

2010 IKSFA Certification,
(L-R) Alex Khasin, Sergey Rachinsky, Sergey Rudnev, Denis Vasilev, Sergey Merkulin
(L-R) Denis Vasilev, Sergey Rudnev, Sergey Merkulin, Sergey Rachinsky

(L-R) Aleksandr Khvostov, Denis Vasilev, Sergey Merkulin

2008 Team Russia, IUKL European Championship. Ventspils, Latvia

2009 European Zone Qualifier for Russian Championship, Team Elec City
2009 IUKL European Championship (L-R) Denis Vasilev, Igor Novikov, Andrey Kravcov

PART 1

1
The Current State Of Kettlebell Sport Methodologies

Kettlebell Sport workshop, 2017 at Orange Kettlebell Club (picture by Nazo)

In Russia, there are many recognized training methods which have successfully produced high-level sportsmen. Unfortunately, very few of these methods are written down and what little documented information exists is inaccessible to the non-Russian speaker. My own training methodology was one of the first translated into English and has been made available to a wider audience.

Kettlebell sport as we know it today has its origins in the 1960's when the first formal set of rules were introduced and kettlebell sport was officially included under the national sports classification of Russia. Afterwards, other USSR republics followed suit and also included it under their own national sport classifications.

Most recognized schools from different regions in Russia

As a result, many countries, specifically particular regions within countries, have formed their own kettlebell sport traditions out of the accumulated experience of several generations. Each different "school" of kettlebell sport has produced its own roster of distinguished champions that grew out of their school's unique training methods. Some of the most recognized schools from the different regions in Russia include Rybinsk, Smolensk, Lipetsk, Kaluga, Blagoveshchensk, Chelyabinsk, Omsk, Tyumen, Tomsk, and of course Saint Petersburg (of which I myself am a product of). It is my hope that as kettlebell sport becomes more popular, the athletes and coaches from these different schools will eventually share their knowledge with the greater public.

I would like to mention one particular textbook published in 2006 which has undoubtedly had the most significant impact on kettlebell sport programming in the recent decade. The title of the book is "Basics of Kettlebell Sport: Teaching Motor Actions and Training Methods". It has earned its status as the most up-to-date manual for kettlebell sport in no small part because of its esteemed contributors, namely Anatoly Sukhovey, Sergey Rudnev, and Evgeny Lopatin, all of whom are legendary figures in kettlebell sport.

Sergey Rudnev is considered by many to be one of the most effective coaches in all of kettlebell sport history. Evgeny Lopatin holds the distinction of being the first male lifter in the sub-60kg weight category to jerk 2x32kg kettlebells 100 times in competition. Vladimir Tikhonov is a sport scientist and practitioner who has attended many high-level competitions and has collected vast amounts of experimental data through his work on beginners and professionals alike.

Unfortunately, the book is only available in the Russian language at the moment. For the benefit of readers in English, I would like to summarize the most important conclusions mentioned in the book that have significantly influenced the trajectory and development of all modern training methods, including my own.

Use of Lighter Training Weights

First, an athlete can progress more safely and efficiently by gradually increasing their kettlebell training weights using 2kg increments. This principle is taken for granted today but back then it was a revolutionary shift in the training process.

Ever since kettlebell sport was born, professional lifters only trained with 32kg to prepare for competition, with the occasional 24kg being used for warm ups (if at all). This made it practically impossible to work on technique and I'm sure it discouraged plenty of promising lifters who couldn't adapt to such a high intensity of work right away. With the introduction of lighter weights, the training process became much more accessible to a larger pool of athletes who could now develop their skills and build their strength in a safe and progressive way.

Professionals also benefited from this change because it allowed them to refine their technique on the lighter weights and this eventually led to higher competition results. The fact that the absolute records for all three competition lifts continues to increase year after year is evidence of its effectiveness. Since then, nearly all the kettlebell schools have incorporated the use of training with lighter kettlebell weights and my method is no exception.

> ***"Unique adaptations also occur in the respiratory system as breathing takes place under special conditions while the kettlebells are resting on the chest... Thus, kettlebell lifters have well-developed respiratory muscles and the average vital capacity (VC) amongst athletes is between 5000 - 5500 mL . Since performing the competition exercises at a high intensity creates an environment of significant oxygen deficiency, the rhythm and depth of breathing are key elements to a successful performance. When the breathing is properly set, the number of breathing cycles exceeds the total number of lifts performed."***

Kettlebell Sport Is A Cyclical Endurance Sport

Second, kettlebell sport is considered a cyclical sport similar to running, biking, skiing, rowing, etc. and should be trained accordingly. Special attention should be given to technique, breathing, and relaxation. The physiological basis of a kettlebell lifter's training consists of progressive functional and structural changes which take place in the body under the influence of the multiple repetitions performed over time with progressively increasing load. The end result is an overall improvement of technique and work capacity.

Competition exercises last up to 10 minutes and are performed at high volume and intensity. It is not uncommon for elite competitors to accumulate more than 7 tons of total weight lifted within the duration of a competition set. To manage such an intense workload, athletes need to have well developed functional abilities, skill, power and strength endurance.

Significant biochemical and morphological changes that take place in the musculoskeletal system include an increase in the volume of individual muscle fibers, improved blood flow to the trained muscles, and a higher concentration of fast twitch fibers. In general, a kettlebell lifter has harmoniously developed organs and muscles with significant hypertrophy of the back extensors, legs and arms.

Unique adaptations also occur in the respiratory system as breathing takes place under special conditions while the kettlebells are resting on the chest. During inhalation in the rack position, the athlete must overcome an additional force equal to the weight of the kettlebells positioned on their torso. Thus, kettlebell lifters have well-developed respiratory muscles and the average vital capacity (VC) amongst professional athletes (Master of Sport and above) is between 5000 - 5500 mL*. Since performing the competition exercises at a high intensity creates an environment of significant oxygen deficiency, the rhythm and depth of breathing are key elements to a successful performance. When the breathing is properly set, the number of breathing cycles exceeds the total number of lifts performed.

Additionally, adaptations to the cardiovascular system are caused by the static and dynamic character of the competition lifts. At no point do the muscles completely relax, even during the rack and overhead position where the lifter stands motionless. This creates an additional obstacle to blood flow thus forcing the cardiac muscle to work harder. The result is a significant hypertrophy of the heart muscle and a higher oxygen carrying capacity of the blood.

* Vital capacity (VC) is a measure of the maximum amount of air that can be inhaled or exhaled during a respiratory cycle. VC for normal adult ranges between 3 to 5 liters.

Classification of Kettlebell Sport Exercises

Third, performing the kettlebell sport competition exercises requires a high level of coordination. During the early stages of training when the formation of motor skills is critical, beginners exhibit excessive stiffness and imprecision in movement which leads to unnecessary energy consumption. As a result, the novice tires quickly and is unable to maintain high quality execution of technique for a prolonged period of time. This is due to the process of excitation spreading over vast areas of the cerebral cortex.

With time and practice, the process of spreading is replaced by concentration. The athlete's movements become more accurate and the resulting relaxation of the opposing muscle groups allows the exercise to be performed at a lower perceived level of effort.

In order to facilitate the process of motor skill mastery, exercises with the kettlebell are divided into three main groups: classic, alternative and auxiliary.

Classic exercises refer to the main competition lifts, namely Jerk, Long Cycle, and Snatch. Experienced athletes spend most of their training volume performing these specific exercises as improvement in competition results generally follows the principle of specific adaptation based on imposed demand. To get better at a particular exercise, the athlete must practice more of that exercise. Success in kettlebell sport is mostly attributed to efficiency of technique rather than overall strength.

Alternative exercises include variations of the main competition lifts such as the one arm jerk, one arm long cycle, multiple hand switches during snatch, double half snatch, double snatch, etc. One benefit of including these exercises in the training program is to supplement and enhance the performance of the classic exercises. They can also provide an alternative for the athlete in case of trauma and injury while maintaining the general motor patterns of kettlebell sport lifting. Additionally, these can be used as a form of active recovery during the training cycle when the athlete is transitioning into the off-season.

Auxiliary exercises are all other exercises which satisfy the specific pedagogical objectives of the training process. These exercises may serve either a special or general developmental purpose. Special auxiliary exercises are meant to develop abilities that are specific to kettlebell sport such as strength, endurance, strength-endurance, and flexibility. General auxiliary exercises are meant to develop broader athletic physical abilities that allow the athlete to tolerate the high volume associated with kettlebell sport training. Besides the development of physical qualities, auxiliary exercises are included to improve posture, develop coordination, improve the regulation of breathing, and to promote relaxation for the stability of the athlete's emotional state.

Summary Principles of Kettlebell Sport Training

The main principles of kettlebell sport training can be generalized into the following five points. After having introduced to you these foundational ideas that underlie nearly all the modern training methods, I will proceed to describe the specifics of my own methodology.

1. The Principle of Gradual Transition (from simple to complex, easy to difficult, light to heavy)

During the training process, it is always best to begin with the least amount of training stimulus necessary to induce a training effect. For experienced athletes, this might mean starting the training cycle with an 8kg or 16kg bell and eventually working up to competition weights. In the case of an absolute novice, the most efficient way to develop the motor patterns for kettlebell sport might be to perform the one arm jerk or long cycle instead of jumping straight into the classic version of the exercises. As their motor skills become more stable, they can gradually transition to working with double bells. Later on they might even increase the weight of both bells.

2. The Principle of Maximum Relaxation and Continuous Breathing

Kettlebell sport lifting is the result of a complex process of coordinated contraction and rapid relaxation of specific muscle groups. Particularly important is the ability to stay relaxed under conditions of general and local fatigue. Inefficient movement leads to unnecessary muscular tension and compensation which accelerates the onset of exhaustion. Improper breathing and breath holding also increases the concentration of anaerobic byproducts in muscle tissue which in turn fuels oxygen debt resulting in a spike in blood pressure and an uncontrolled increase in the heart rate.

The athlete's highest priority therefore is to develop the ability to quickly contract and relax the working muscles as well as to gain mastery of their breathing. It is by no accident that the speed of neuromuscular conduction and the ability to control one's breathing are the main qualities which distinguish elite athletes from mediocre lifters.

3. The Principle of Periodization and Training Cyclicity

The training process for kettlebell sport should follow the general principles of periodized training. This means that the athlete's programming should clearly reflect the specific training goals associated with the macro, meso, and micro cycles. Later in the book I go into much greater detail about the use of strategic and tactical planning in the training process.

4. The Principle of Muscular Interdependence

As with any specialized physical activity, there tends to be a general set of musculoskeletal adaptations that are unique to the activity performed. In the case of kettlebell sport lifting, the development of the primary extensor muscles generally outpaces the development of the flexors. In some cases, the disproportionate muscle growth between the left and right parts of the body can also impede performance and might lead to chronic injury. A sound training program should therefore include general exercises that are aimed to reduce these muscular imbalances.

5. The Principle of SAID

According to the principle of specific adaptation based on imposed demands, success in kettlebell sport cannot be achieved without direct practice of the classic exercises. A large part of the training process must be devoted to the practice and development of the specific skills mentioned above in order to produce a highly skilled and capable athlete.

2
My Training Methodology

In 2005 I moved from my hometown of Kaliningrad to Saint Petersburg. I already had my Master of Sport rank in kettlebell sport and mistakenly thought that I would be content with my professional achievement. I resolved to keep myself in shape by lifting weights and thought no more about pursuing kettlebell sport. Before long I began to miss participating in competitions and by 2006 I was already thinking about making my comeback. The following year I started looking for a coach who could lead me back into kettlebell sport and that's when I met Arkady Semyonov, who was himself accomplished as an Honored Master of Sport. We started working together and after a few months I was able to perform 83 repetitions with 2x32kg in the Long Cycle event at the Championship of Leningrad Oblast. This earned me the rank of Master of Sport International Class and it was good enough to attract the attention of the legendary Sergey Rachinsky.

Sergey had already retired as a professional athlete with the distinction of being an undefeated 9-time World Champion. I had heard a lot about his victories and unique competition tactics and I wanted him to coach me more than anything else. As it happened, he accepted me as his student and the rest was history. After 9 months of training under him, I became the Long Cycle Champion of Europe in the 85kg weight class and exceeded the numbers required for Master of Sport International Class. This was an auspicious start because during the succeeding 8 years as a member of the Russian National Team I was undefeated in competition and became a 7-time Russian Champion, 7-time European Champion, and 6-time World Champion.

The methodology I am about to describe was born out of the analysis of my own training plans that were created by Sergey. Since 2009, I began to train my own students with the same methodology and their own high results have confirmed the effectiveness of this method. The main features of the method that Sergey passed on to me are the following:

Each sportsman is unique and the specific approach to training must be individual.

Short-term planning of 3 sessions, with each week building on the previous week.

Moderate volume per session, focusing on high intensity and a high-speed finish.

Ten Principles of Kettlebell Sport Programming

1. When first learning about kettlebell sport, begin with Long Cycle rather than Biathlon (Jerk and Snatch)

I came to this conclusion for several reasons. First, it is much less stressful and therefore more effective to learn one new exercise at a time. The Jerk and Snatch complement each other because the Jerk doesn't require a swing and the Snatch doesn't require a Jerk. The Long Cycle has both these elements in one exercise but it has the distinction of being performed at a slower rate* of lifting which allows you to focus on perfecting your technique.

Attention to technique is of paramount importance when you are just starting out in kettlebell sport. As kettlebell sport is categorized as a cyclical endurance sport (similar to running, biking, and swimming) where the body goes through a fixed set of movements over time, it is important to realize that the overall number of mistakes compounds with every small inefficiency in technique. The higher the rate of repetitions, the potential for mistakes increases, your perceived effort skyrockets, fatigue sets in, and your performance suffers which affects your target end result. As a consequence, lifters decrease their work pace due to generalized exhaustion or completely stop and terminate their set prematurely due to localized fatigue (such as the forearms during Snatch).

Second, based on my experiences and from observing my students, learning Long Cycle first makes learning Biathlon much more rewarding and less frustrating. Of all the kettlebell sport lifts, I consider Long Cycle to be the most natural from a biomechanical point of view as it affords you more opportunities for relaxation compared to the Biathlon exercises. Instead of jumping straight into Jerk where you won't have the opportunity to reset your Rack Position with a Clean while your technique isn't great yet, you will be able to practice your Top Fixation and your Drop Into The Rack with significantly less stress. Additionally, the shorter amplitude of the Clean will allow you to improve your understanding of the Swing while avoiding the pain of having pumped forearms from performing hundreds of poorly executed snatches. Additionally, Long Cycle requires more strength compared to Jerk and Snatch and I consider this a good thing because this will allow you to build a much more solid foundation for general physical development.

---

*By slower, I am referring to the fact that the target numbers for Long Cycle are much lower compared to Biathlon (Jerk and Snatch). As an example let us compare the requirements for Master of Sport rank in the 85kg weight class: Long Cycle - 78 repetitions, Biathlon - 215 points (roughly 130 repetitions in Jerk and 170 repetitions in Snatch). Since the regulation time is 10min, Long Cycle is performed at a rate of 7.8 repetitions per minute (rpm) while the Jerk must be performed at an average pace of 13rpm and Snatch at 17rpm. As we can see, Long Cycle is the slowest lift and Snatch is the fastest. Long Cycle is more forgiving to lifting technique imperfections while Snatch is the most sensitive and fragile.

2. Build skills and technique first, complete a 10min set with stable technique second, chase repetitions and results third

UNDERSTAND THE SEQUENCE OF YOUR TARGETS

FIRST
Establish an initial skill and understanding of the lifting technique

SECOND
Manage 10 minutes non-stop set with a stable lifting technique

THIRD
Chasing maximum reps according to the competition rules and regulations.

Fig. 1 Sequence of Targets

It is vital to build a solid foundation before pursuing any high level goals in kettlebell sport. Whether it be for maintenance of your physical fitness or for competitive lifting, being able to execute efficient technique is the only way to ensure your safety and progress. As such, you will first need to show sufficient mastery of the following phases in each discipline:

For Long Cycle

Clean ➡ Rack Position ➡ First Dip ➡ Bump ➡ Second Dip ➡ Top Fixation ➡ Drop to Rack ➡ Drop to Back Swing

For Jerk

Rack Position ➡ First Dip ➡ Bump ➡ Second Dip ➡ Top Fixation ➡ Drop to Rack

For Snatch

Back Swing ➡ Swing Forward ➡ Acceleration + Pull ➡ Overhead Catch ➡ Top Fixation ➡ Drop to Back Swing

After you are able to demonstrate proficiency in each of the phases mentioned above, you can attempt a 10 minute set without setting the bells down on the floor. For Long Cycle and Jerk, your goal should be to rest in the Rack Position and in Top Fixation to complete the set. For Snatch, you should try to perform the set with only one hand switch. At this point, your attention should be on staying as relaxed as possible in order to maintain your technique at a stable pace from start to end. Completing a 10 minute set will give you confidence to approach the next step which is to increase the number of repetitions you can perform.

Since kettlebell sport achievements are classified according to sport ranking tables (where Rank 3 is the lowest and Honored Master of Sport is the highest level of achievement), you can objectively measure your progress by looking at how much you have increased your sport rank. As an example, you can order your targets in the following way:

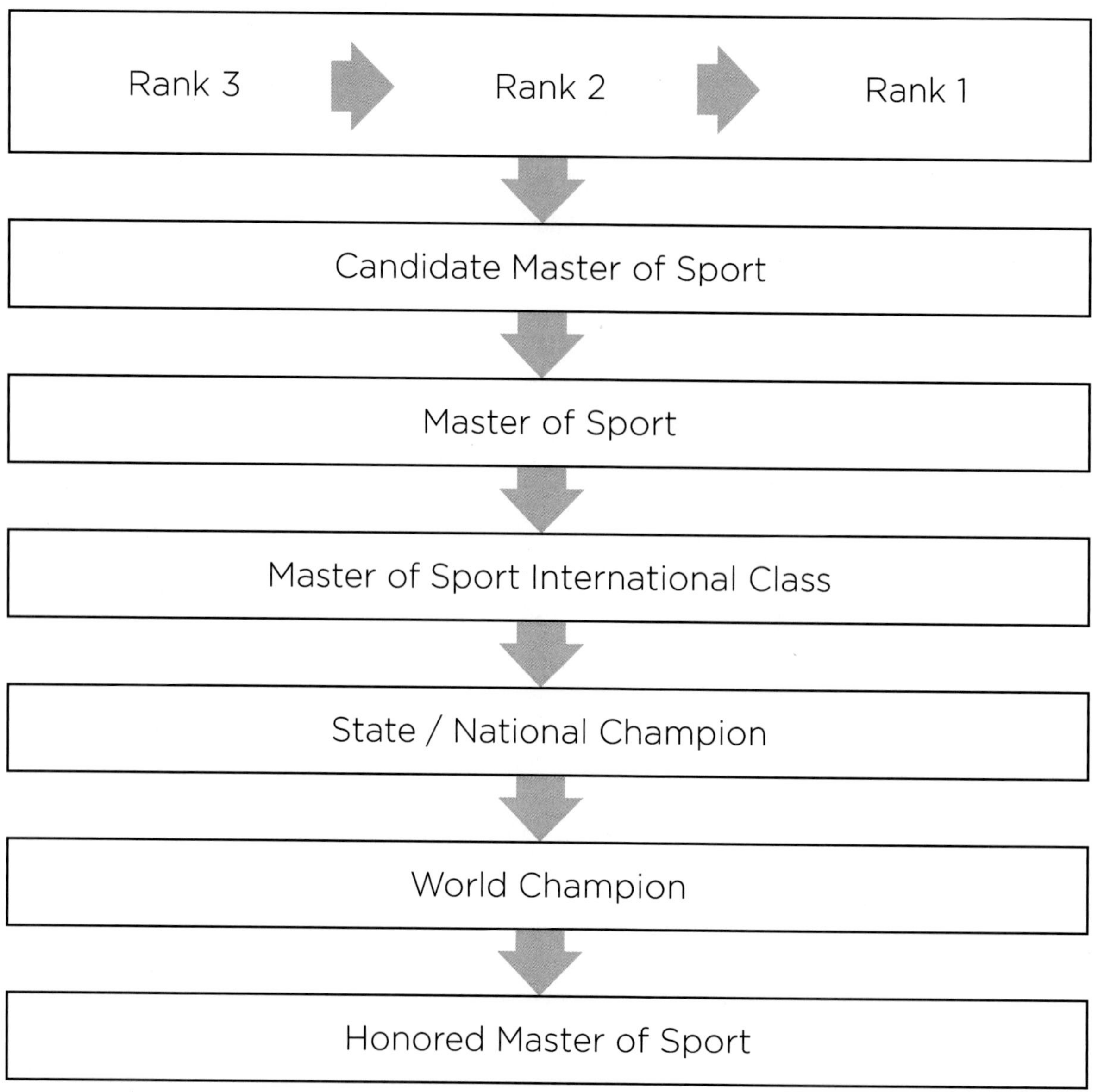

These targets can be achieved by "developing the necessary physical qualities (both general and specific endurance, strength, flexibility, and agility), forming the specific skills of competing on the platform (integral training), and focusing on the upbringing of mental, psychic, and volitional qualities which provide positive reaction of the organism to stress-factors of competitive activity".
(Muminov V.I., 1995)

3. Gradual increase of kettlebell training weights in no more than 2kg increments.

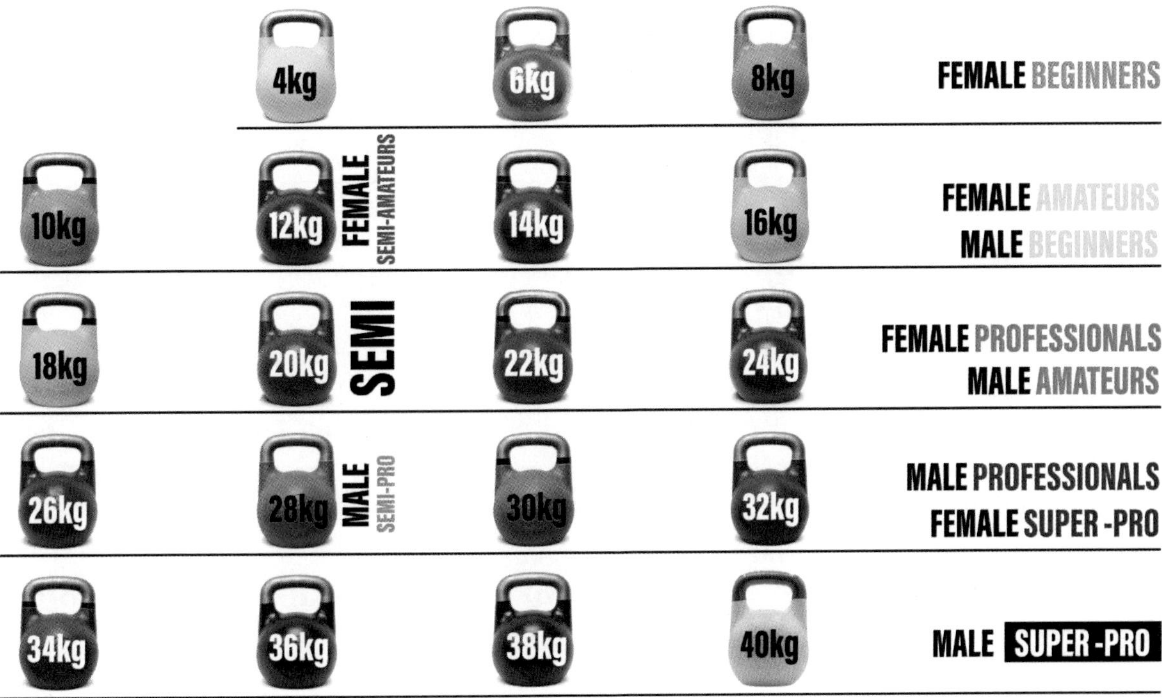

Fig. 2. Kettlebell weights

Generally speaking, I've found that men can train with bells between 12-32kg, women with 6-24kg, and children between the ages of 10-12 years old can start training with 4kg. Going back to my previous point of properly arranging your training targets, training with lighter bells will always be a good investment of your time while you are still developing your lifting technique. Keep in mind that "lighter" is a relative term because, as an example, for a male beginner the 10kg might be light and 16kg might be heavy while for a male professional 24kg is light and 32kg is heavy. Once you are confident with your level of technique, you can start to move to the heavier bells using the following chart as your guide.

10-minute set			What it means
Long Cycle	Jerk (x1,5)	Snatch (x2)	
less than 60 reps	less than 90 reps	less than 120 reps	too heavy, go lighter
60-70 reps	90-105 reps	120-140 reps	it's heavy, but solid
70-80 reps	105-120 reps	140-160 reps	it's solid, can go 2kg heavier
80-100 reps	120-150 reps	160-200 reps	rock solid number, can go 4kg higher
100-120 reps	150-180 reps	200-240 reps	this kettlebell weight is not too hard for you
over 120 reps	180 reps	240 reps	this kettlebell weight is too light for you

4. Use of Interval, Repetitive, Competition, Flat, Variable, Time Pyramids and Ladders during training sessions

Each of these training methods, and their variations, is an independent instrument for solving specific training tasks at a particular moment during the training cycle. They are meant to be viewed as tools that are meant to develop the particular physical and mental qualities necessary for successful competition performance. All these methods will be discussed in great detail later in the book.

5. Each training session contains about 10 minutes on average of total lifting time per exercise, and each training cycle lasts from anywhere between 5 to 12 weeks

Since the regulation time during competitions is 10 minutes, the total volume of lifting time while training for each lift should reflect this duration.

6. Training pace should always be at competition pace or slightly faster, never slower

Because the total volume of lifting is restricted to about 10 minutes, my method focuses on achieving higher intensity through manipulation of pace rather than weight or time.

7. Only 1 kettlebell weight should be used per session

Other methods use increasing or decreasing kettlebell weights within one session. My training method only requires one weight of bells during the training session and the weights increase progressively over the following weeks. The exception to this rule is that you can use heavier bells on cleans and swings during long cycle and snatch. For example, if your main long cycle sets are 24kg you can do an additional set of cleans with 26kg.

8. The workout load can be adjusted through manipulation of time, weight, rest, and pace

Depending on what factors are present (physical or mental status of the athlete, where you are in the training cycle, overall experience, etc), session of one kettlebell sport exercise can be low volume (less than 10 min of lifting total), full volume (10 min of lifting total), extended volume (greater than 10 min of lifting total), each session can be further adjusted by increasing or decreasing the weight of the kettlebells (±1-2kg), the time of rest between sets (±1-2min), and the lifting pace (±1-2rpm(repetitions per minute).

9. The very last minute of each workout should be the fastest

This develops the discipline of building up the pace gradually during the working sets. By learning how to start slow and end fast (with each minute as fast as or slightly faster than the minute before it), you will avoid one of the biggest mistakes in kettlebell lifting where you are unable to complete your set because you exhausted yourself prematurely. During every workout, we are practicing how to accelerate by always finishing with at least 1 repetition above the target pace. Kettlebell sport is an endurance sport and finishing strong is more important than being unable to complete the set.

10. You should always do a 10 minute set at least once a month

Being able to handle a 10 minute set is a specific skill. This means that you get better at it by completing more 10 minute sets over the span of your career. This does not mean that you should attempt a 10 minute set with competition weights every month. You can and should, however, use lighter training weights during your test sets. You can also compete in other events that are not specific to your main discipline. For example, you have the option to do a 10 minute set of cleans only with lighter bells if you feel that you really need to work on your clean technique. Or you could also go for a lighter 10 minute Biathlon competition to support a local event. In either case, you are able to build the specific skill of handling 10 minutes without the overwhelming stress and pressure of competing in your main discipline.

Structuring Your Own Kettlebell Sport Program

> ***... it will be extremely beneficial to have at least one other person (whether it be a teammate or a coach) who can lead and guide you through the tougher training sessions.***

One of the best things about training for kettlebell sport is that it is extremely modest with regard to training environment and equipment. It's possible to follow a professional program with only one square meter of space and two kettlebells at the bare minimum. Training can be done almost anywhere and plenty of athletes have completed their training cycles by lifting in their kitchens, garages, living rooms, and back yards. It is a sport that can be practiced alone if need be.

However, I must mention that as your level and ability increases and the more challenging the workouts become, it will be extremely beneficial to have at least one other person (whether it be a teammate or a coach) who can lead and guide you through the tougher training sessions. Ideally, you should train with a group of athletes with equal or greater experience than you. Such a group provides better motivation and courage as all the members are learning through shared experience. The atmosphere of having a team with you also makes training more interesting and exciting. If there is no opportunity to train regularly together, you should at least try to do your most important training sessions with a group.

It is also important to keep a record of your own training to have better control of your preparedness, health, and physical development. The more details of your own training you can capture and write down, the more accurate your programming and projection of target results. A training journal is indispensable when it comes to objective self-evaluation, especially when you are deciding whether you can push yourself harder or temporarily pull back. Here is an example of my own spreadsheet which I use to track my own workouts.

day	Long Cycle / Jerk				Cleans / Snatch				GPP
	KB weight	**kind of work**	**pace**	**completed**	**KB weight**	**kind of work**	**pace**	**competed**	
January 2021									
2	LC 32kg	1', 2', 3', 1' (2', 3', 2' rest)	9-12 rpm	10 / 10, 11 / 10, 11, 12 / 14					Back Squats 145lb/(1'w+1'r) x 3sets (22/24/26), Running 4 rounds (11'12"60)
3									
4									

5	LC 32kg	1' x 5 (1' rest)	12-14 rpm	14 / 14 / 14 / 14/ 15	Cleans 32kg	1' x 2 (1' rest)	12-14 rpm	13 / 18	Back Squats 145lb/60rp(2'36"), Push ups 20rp x 2sets, Running 6 rounds (17'55"33)
6									
7	LC 32kg	3' x 2 (5' rest)	9-12 rpm	10, 11, 12 / 12, 12, 14	Cleans 32kg	3' (5' rest)	12-14 rpm	12, 12, 19 total 43r	Back Squats 145lb/ (1'w+1'r) x 4sets (25/25/25/26), Push ups 30rp, Running 8 rounds (23'08"08)
8									
9	LC 32kg	5'	9-12 rpm	12, 12, 12, 12, 12 total 60r	Cleans 32kg	1' x 2 (1' rest)	12-14 rpm	13 / 15	Back Squats 145lb/80rp(3'39"), Push ups 20rp x 3sets, Running 4 rounds (12'29"33)
10									

Fig. 3. Sample training spreadsheet

Now, I will introduce you to the different training methods in kettlebell sport before going into the details of Strategic and Tactical Planning.

Training Methods in Kettlebell Sport

There are six main training methods in my kettlebell sport methodology. Each method follows particular guidelines in order to bring about a specific adaptation. As such, your workout may contain only one training method or it can include a mix of several methods.

1. Interval Method

Purpose: This method is used for developing speed-endurance and strength-endurance. This type of lifting performed at maximum intensity works best for experienced athletes who already have stable technique and want to increase their competition pace. On the other hand, using this kind of workout for beginners with low intensity will allow them to improve their lifting technique.

Intensity (Pace): 100-150% of target competition pace.

Volume: 2-10 sets of 1-5 minutes each; up to 12 minutes of total work. The duration of all the sets must be the same: all 1 minute sets, all 2 minute sets, etc. Maximum volume is used in the Base and Check-Preparatory mesocycles. Minimum volume is used in the Draw-in and Pre-Competition mesocycles*.

Rest: Rest time between sets is limited and fixed, usually equal to the time of work. If the workout feels too hard or easy, the rest time can be extended or lessened by 1 minute.

---

* See next section: 2.2.2 Strategic Planning

$$T_{rest} = T_{work} \pm 1 \text{ minute}$$
(ex. 1-2 minutes rest = 1 minute work ± 1 minute)

Unique Features: Using this method results in an intensification of the training process with it's large total tonnage (up to 1.5 times higher total volume than other training methods). It is also an excellent method for developing resistance to physical and mental stress. The organism is forced to perform in an oxygen-deprived state, thus improving the body's oxygen-carrying capabilities.

Sub-methods: Interval-Flat (steady lifting pace), Interval-Variable (flexible lifting pace), Interval-Time Pyramid and Ladders (varying duration of work sets with very short rest periods).

2 Repetitive Method

Purpose: This method is used for developing speed-strength, strength, and speed. It is highly effective for improving and stabilizing lifting technique

Intensity (Pace): 110-150% of target competition pace.

Volume: 2-4 sets of 2-5 minutes each; up to 15 minutes of total work. The duration of all the sets must be the same: all 2 minute sets, all 3 minute sets, etc. Maximum volume is used in the Base and Check-Preparatory mesocycles. Minimum volume is used in the Draw-in and Pre-competition mesocycles.

Rest: Rest time is limited but allows for full recovery between sets. Recovery between sets can be extended up to 10 minutes when absolutely necessary in order to complete the workout. If the workout feels too easy, the lifting pace can be increased by 1-2 repetitions per minute.

$$T_{rest} = T_{work} \times 1.5\text{-}2$$
(ex. 3-4 minutes rest = 2 minutes work x 1.5-2)

Unique Features: This method increases the total time of work done (up to 1.5 times longer) compared to other methods. It emphasizes endurance and accuracy of technique development while also strengthening the muscles and tendons.

Sub-methods: Repetitive-Flat (steady lifting pace), Repetitive-Variable (flexible lifting pace), Repetitive-Time Pyramid and Ladders (varying duration of work sets with a comfortable amount of rest in between).

3 Competition Method

Purpose: This method is used to develop the base qualities needed for physical and mental preparedness specific to kettlebell sport. Performance is graded on the best possible result, which is the maximum number of repetitions performed within a given time period.

Intensity (Pace): 100-200% of competition pace.
The shorter the set, the faster the pace.

Volume: 1 set of 1-8 minutes. Sets lasting only 1-2 minutes are rarely used by experienced athletes, and even then only under the conditions of stable lifting technique. The goal is to increase the target competition pace. Sets lasting between 3-8 minutes are more commonly used. For beginners, it is recommended to stay close to the target competition pace throughout the set in order to develop solid lifting technique. Longer duration sets are used in the Check-Preparatory mesocycle and the Competing microcycle. Shorter sets are used in the Base and Pre-Competition mesocycles. Usually, the competition method workout is the final workout in each microcycle.

Rest: None.

Unique Features: This method develops overall competition preparedness by testing all of your abilities with the goal of executing a winning performance.

Sub-methods: Competition-Flat (steady lifting pace), Competition-Variable (flexible lifting pace).

4 Flat Method

Purpose: This method is used to develop the aerobic abilities of the athlete. Maximum intensity works best for experienced athletes who already have stable technique and want to increase their target competition pace. Low intensity works best for beginners who are still developing their lifting technique.

Intensity (Pace): 100-140% of target competition pace. The chosen pace must be maintained throughout the set from the first minute until the last.

Volume: 1 set of 4-12 minutes. It is possible to use lighter or heavier than competition kettlebell weights during this type of workout. Sets lasting 8 minutes and longer can be performed with lighter weights, while sets lasting 7 minutes and shorter can be performed with heavier weights.

Rest: None.

Unique Features: This method stimulates adaptation to monotonous work and builds focus against distractions. It also develops endurance and accuracy of technique while forcing the athlete to maintain a stable heart rate.

Sub-methods: The Flat Method can be used as a tool to modify your lifting pace. Flat-Interval (multiple sets, short rest time), Flat-Repetitive (multiple sets, comfortable rest time), Flat-Competitive (one set with competition weights), Flat-Time Pyramid and Ladders (multiple sets of different duration).

5 Variable Method

Purpose: This method is used to improve special-endurance. It also allows the athlete to work on their competition pace strategy. This method is used in all stages of the training cycle.

Intensity (Pace): 80-160% of target competition pace. The pace may vary throughout the set depending on the chosen strategy. Here are some examples that all equal to 90 repetitions in 10 minutes:

"slow start - fast finish" (8,8,8,8,8,9,10,10,10,11)
"fast start - slow finish" (10,10,10,10,10,8,8,8,8,8)
"slow - fast wave" (8,10,8,10,8,10,8,10,8,10)
"strong start - slow middle - strong finish" (9,9,9,9,8,8,8,9,9,12)

There are many more combinations of similar strategies which I have not included here. Whichever strategy you choose, it must be determined in advance prior to the set and must be executed accordingly.

Volume: 1 set of 4-12 minutes. It is possible to use lighter or heavier than competition kettlebell weights during this type of workout. Sets lasting 8 minutes and longer can be performed with lighter weights, while sets lasting 7 minutes and shorter can be performed with heavier weights.

Rest: None.

Unique Features: This method breaks up the monotony of lifting at a particular pace. The varying pace presents a unique challenge to the athlete by forcing them to maintain stable technique while constantly changing pace. It also exercises the athlete's tactical thinking by pushing them to adjust their breathing and relaxation accordingly. These types of workouts are great at developing contrast work adaptation (being able to switch intensities on the spot). It also serves as a mental game for the athlete by making them come up with their own strategies to successfully complete the set.

Sub-methods: The variable method can be used to finely tune your preferred lifting pace strategy. Variable-Interval (multiple sets with short rest), Variable-Repetitive (multiple sets with comfortable rest), Variable-Competitive (one set with competition weights), Variable-Time Pyramids and Ladders (multiple sets of different durations).

6 Time Pyramid and Ladders Method

Purpose: If the rest periods are short, this method can be used to develop speed-endurance and strength-endurance (similar to the Interval method). If the rest periods are comfortable, this method can be used to develop speed-strength, strength, and speed (similar to the Repetitive method). The time pyramid is effective for improving and stabilizing lifting technique.

Intensity (Pace): 100-140% of target competition pace.

Volume: 3-5 sets of 1-4 minutes each; up to 10 minutes of total work. Whatever the type of time pyramid or ladder you are using, the total time of work should be 10 minutes or close to it: "time pyramid" (1,2,3,2,1 minutes), "descending ladder" (4,3,2,1 minutes), "ascending ladder" (1,2,3,4 minutes). Maximum volume is used during the Base and Check-Preparatory mesocycles. Minimum volume is used during the Draw-in and Pre-Competition mesocycles.

Rest: Recovery between sets can follow the rules of the Interval or Repetitive method, depending on the athlete's needs.

Unique Features: The pyramid and ladders structure breaks up the monotony of a fixed training session. It develops lifting technique and concentration under the changing duration of the sets. It also serves as a mental game for the athlete by making them come up with their own strategies to successfully complete the set.

Sub-methods: Time Pyramid and Ladder-Interval, Flat/Variable (short rest time, steady or flexible lifting pace), Time Pyramid and Ladder-Repetitive, Flat/Variable (comfortable rest time, steady or flexible lifting pace).

Sample Table of Training Methods

Below is a sample table for either Jerk or Long Cycle containing all the various training methods as well as the recommended pace per minute to achieve 100 repetitions (pace 10) in 10 minutes. You can construct a similar table for yourself by multiplying your target pace with the percentages found in each cell. For example, if your target pace is 15 then your average pace per minute when using the Interval method should be 21 (140% x 15, 1 minute x 5-10 sets), 19.5 (2 minutes x 3-5 sets), 18 (3 minutes x 2-4 sets), 16.5 (110% x 15, 4 minutes x 2-3 sets), and 15 (100% x 15, 5 minutes x 2 sets) respectively.

In general, the shorter the training sets, the faster the lifting pace. The slowest pace is the actual competition set while the fastest pace can be found during the intervals (up to 200% of competition pace). The total volume of time per training session will vary depending on which part of the mesocycle the athlete is in. The concepts of macrocycle, mesocycle, and microcycle will be discussed in the following chapter but for take it for now that low volume (5-9 minutes total) is used in the Draw-in and Pre-competition mesocycle, full volume (10 minutes total) is used during the Check-preparatory mesocycle and Competing microcycle, and extended volume (greater than 10 minutes total) is used during the Base and Check-preparatory mesocycles.

Now that we've gone through all the training methods, we can turn our attention to Strategic and Tactical Planning. The next two sections will allow us to put together a training program using the elements we've just covered.

TRAINING METHOD	TRAINING SET TIME FRAMES											
	1 min	2 min	3 min	4 min	5 min	6 min	7 min	8 min	9 min	10 min	11 min	12 min
Interval method	x5-10 sets	x3-5 sets	x2-4 sets	x2-3 sets	x2 sets							
pace in rpm	**14**	**13**	**12**	**11**	**19**					**10**		
intensity in percentage	140%	130%	120%	110%	100%							
Repetitive method		x2-4 sets	x2-4 sets	x2-3 sets	x2-3 sets							
pace in rpm		**14**	**13**	**12**	**11**					**10**		
intensity in percentage		140%	130%	120%	110%							
Flat method				x1 set	x1 set	x1 set	x1 set	x1 set	x1 set	x1 set	x1 set	
pace in rpm				**10-14**	**10-14**	**10-13**	**8-13**	**8-12**	**6-12**	**6-12**	**6-12**	
intensity in percentage				up to 140%	up to 140%	up to 130%	up to 130%	up to 120%	up to 120%	up to 120%	up to 120%	
Variable method			x1 set	x1 set	x1 set	x1 set	x1 set	x1 set	x1 set	x1 set		
pace in rpm			**10-16**	**10-14**	**10-14**	**10-13**	**8-12**	**8-12**	**6-12**	**6-12**	**6-12**	
intensity in percentage			up to 160%	up to 140%	up to 140%	up to 130%	up to 130%	up to 120%	up to 120%	up to 120%	up to 120%	
Competing method	x1 set	x1 set	x1 set	x1 set	x1 set	x1 set	x1 set	x1 set				
pace in rpm	**18-12**	**16-17**	**15**	**13-14**	**12**	**11-12**	**11**	**10-11**		**10**		
intensity in percentage	120-180%	160-170%	150%	130-140%	120%	110-120%	110%	100-110%		100%		

Time Pyramid	1min work	2min work		3min work			2min work		1min work		
performed either in Interval or Repetitive methods	**10-12**	**10-12**	**10-12**	**10-12**	**10-12**	**10-14**	**10-12**	**10-12**	**12-14**		**pace in rpm**
	100-120%	100-120%	100-120%	100-120%	100-120%	100-140%	100-120%	100-120%	120-140%		**intensity pecentage**
Time Ladder DOWN	4min work				3min work			2min work		1min work	
performed either in Interval or Repetitive methods	**10-12**	**10-12**	**10-12**	**10-12**	**10-12**	**10-12**	**12-14**	**10-12**	**12-14**	**12-14**	**pace in rpm**
	100-120%	100-120%	100-120%	100-120%	100-120%	100-120%	120-140%	100-120%	120-140%	120-140%	**intensity pecentage**
Time Ladder UP	1min work	2min work		3min work			4min work				
performed either in Interval or Repetitive methods	**10-12**	**10-12**	**10-12**	**10-12**	**10-12**	**10-12**	**10-12**	**10-12**	**10-12**	**12-14**	**pace in rpm**
	100-120%	100-120%	100-120%	100-120%	100-120%	100-120%	100-120%	100-120%	100-120%	120-140%	**intensity pecentage**

Fig. 4. Jerk/Long Cycle pace table

Strategic Planning

Strategic planning simply refers to dividing up the calendar year into training cycles depending on which competitions (or personal tests) you plan on doing. Depending on your country of residence, the most important events which dominate the competition calendar might include the National Championships, Regional Championships (Asian, European, American, Oceanian, etc), and the World Championships. Gaps between competitions should be used as a preparatory period. During these weeks, you can join secondary competitions and schedule mock competition sets in the gym.

Correct strategic planning also takes into account all the extraneous factors surrounding an athlete's life such as their personal life, business plans, family responsibilities, school, etc. Consistently being able to balance all these elements will secure good health, longevity, and a higher chance of success of achieving training goals. As part of the strategic plan, each training cycle should have meaning and purpose. Strategic planning thus refers to identifying realistic targets and developing a plan to reach them during the actual training program. The goal is to lead an athlete towards the peak of their physical and mental capabilities within a predetermined time frame within the context of a macrocycle, mesocycle, and microcycle.

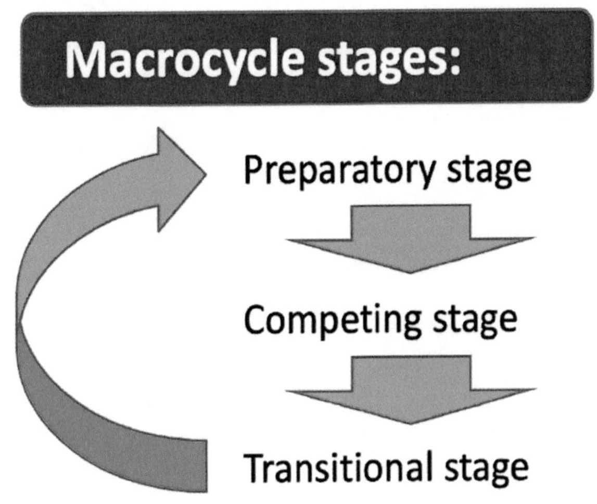

Fig. 5. Macrocycle stages

A macrocycle refers to several training cycles which lead up to the main competition. For example, if the main competition is the annual World Championships then the macrocycle duration for this particular period is one year. Conversely, in Olympic sports, their macrocycle lasts for four years.

The Preparatory stage is when you are focused on achieving your best physical condition in your main specialization. This stage may consist of one or two training cycles depending on the schedule of your competition calendar.

The Competing stage is when you are actually lifting during competitions.

The Transitional stage is when you are actively resting from your main specialization. This might mean changing exercises (from Long Cycle to Biathlon), switching to lighter weights on the same exercise (from 32kg to 24kg in Long Cycle), or changing exercises and using lighter weights (from 32kg Long Cycle to 24kg Biathlon).

A complete training cycle lasts four to twelve weeks and is composed of multiple mesocycles which last approximately two to six weeks each. During this time, secondary tournaments can be used as preparation for the main competition. Beginners with no experience can prepare for their first 10 minute set with light kettlebells within four to five weeks while advanced athletes can do test sets with lighter than competition weights at the end of each mesocycle. As an example, when I start my Biathlon preparation for 32kg my Draw-in mesocycle for Jerk lasts about 2-4 weeks and I usually start with 16kg and 20kg. By the end of this mesocycle, I already feel prepared enough to do a fun competition with 24kg and get a feel of how the first stage of my preparation went. I can then use the feedback I get to calibrate and plan for the next stage of my training.

The Draw-in mesocycle is two to three weeks long and consists of the Recovery/Maintaining microcycles. The longest mesocycle is the Base mesocycle which lasts for four to six weeks and includes the Laborious, Refining, and Recovery/Maintaining microcycles.

The Check-preparatory mesocycle is two to three weeks long and consists of the Laborious, Refining, and Recovery/Maintaining microcycles.

The Pre-competition mesocycle phase is short, usually not exceeding two weeks, and consists of Refining and Recovery/Maintaining microcycles.

As mentioned earlier, depending on which phase of the mesocycle the athlete is in, the total duration of work can be low (5-9 minutes), full (10 minutes), or extended (more than 10 minutes). Low volume is common during the Draw-in and Pre-competition mesocycle while full volume is common during the Check-preparatory mesocycle and Competing microcycle. Extended volume is generally seen during the Base and Check-preparatory mesocycles.

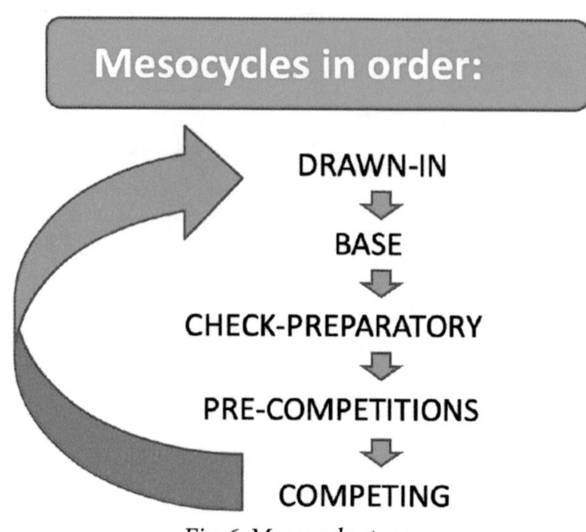

Fig. 6. Mesocycle stages

Mesocycles are again divided into more immediate days and weeks of training and this group of sessions is called a microcycle. Each microcycle can last between two to seven days. This group of daily training sessions are what athletes typically recognize when talking about a training program.

The Draw-in microcycle is the lightest cycle where you are progressing from lighter training weights towards the heavier competition weights. The total time of work per training and training pace is low to medium.

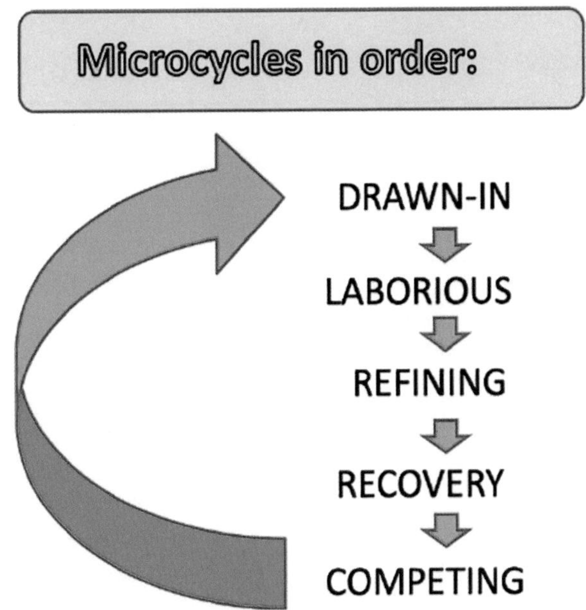

Fig. 7. Microcycle stages

The Laborious microcycle is the hardest part of the cycle where the toughest training sessions are carried out. The total time of work is high and the pace is near maximum during each session. This is the time where you are growing into the next level of your performance.

The Refining microcycle is when the total volume of work drops but the high working pace is maintained. The focus during this time is on the development of your aerobic capacities while maintaining perfection of technique. This is when you are getting into your best shape.

The Recovery microcycle consists of only a few training sessions and it can be done either after the Refining microcycle or after the Competing microcycle. The volume of work is minimal and the work pace is moderate because the goal of this period is to facilitate your physical and mental recovery. If done after a Refining microcycle, you will feel fresh and strong during competition. If performed after a Competing microcycle, it can be used as a reset to start getting ready for a new training cycle.

The Competing microcycle includes the actual days of competition. Kettlebell Sport competitions last anywhere between one to three days. Athletes who sign up for Long Cycle only compete one day while Biathlon participants might be lifting over a span of two days.

Below is an example of the strategic plan I implemented leading up to the World Championships in 2014. The main challenge during this particular cycle was that I only had twenty days between the European Championships on May 14 and the Russian Championships on June 3. I needed to defend my title at both events in order to qualify for the Russian National Team which would secure my entry to the World Championships in November. Instead of having two separate cycles where I could reset to lighter weights, I had to structure my plan to keep myself in peak shape for both championships. Twenty days was not enough time to go back to lighter kettlebells so I kept training with 32kg but I limited the intensity to 80% effort. I kept my volume moderate, maintained my training at competition pace, emphasized cardio and mobility, and kept a strict sleep schedule for recovery. In the end, my plan worked and I was able to get 91 repetitions at the European Championships and 89 repetitions at the Russian Championships.

Dates		Mesocycles	Microcycles	Events / Competition
2013	Nov	Draw-in	Recovery	Nov 23, IUKL WC-13
	Dec		Draw-in	
			Laborious	Jan 11, EF Cup
2014	Jan		Competing	
		Check-preparatory	Draw-in	
			Laborious	
	Feb		Refining	Feb 23, CaliOpen
		Check-preparatory / Base / Pre-competition	Competing	
	Mar		Recovery	
			Draw-in	
	Apr		Laborious	
			Refining	May 14, EC
	May		Competing	
		Pre-competition	Recovery	
			Refining	Jun 3, RC
	Jun	Draw-in	Competing	
			Recovery	
			Draw-in	
	Jul	Pre-competition	Laborious	
			Refining	Aug 3, Bay Area
	Aug		Competing	
		Check-preparatory	Draw-in	
			Laborious	Sep 29, Local Comp
	Sep		Refining	
		Check-preparatory / Base / Pre-competition	Competing	
	Oct		Recovery	
			Draw-in	
	Nov		Laborious	
			Refining	Nov 23, WC-14
			Competing	

Macrocycle in 2014 (from the World Championship 2013 until the World Championship 2014)

by Denis Vasilev, MSIC
Multiple World Champion
(LC, 85kg weight class)

Fig. 8. 2014 World Championships Macrocycle

Tactical Planning

The three main competition disciplines in kettlebell sport are Long Cycle, Biathlon (Jerk and Snatch), and Triathlon (Long Cycle, Jerk, and Snatch). When training for Long Cycle or Biathlon exclusively, it is generally accepted that you don't include any discipline that isn't your current specialization. For example, if you are training for a serious Long Cycle result you shouldn't be doing any Jerk or Snatch sets during your training cycle and vice versa. The exception to this rule is if you are competing in Triathlon which includes all three lifts. During this cycle, your main training sets should consist of Jerk and Snatch with the occasional set of Cleans. It is acceptable to perform a Long Cycle training session once a week or once every two weeks.

Long Cycle

Fig. 9. Kettlebell Sport Events

Whichever your chosen discipline, I recommend lifting thrice a week. The most common schedules are the "type I fixed" (Mon-Wed-Fri or Tue-Thu-Sat) and the "type II floating" (7 total workouts in 2 weeks, lifting every other day).

Training schedule variations		Mo	Tu	We	Th	Fr	Sa	Su	Mo	Tu	We	Th	Fr	Sa	Su
I	a	KB		KB		KB			KB		KB		KB		
	b		KB		KB		KB			KB		KB		KB	
II		KB		KB		KB		KB		KB		KB		KB	

Fig. 10. Weekly training schedule

Inconsistency is the biggest issue that prevents an athlete from succeeding! For a professional kettlebell athlete, at least three workouts a week provides the necessary volume to stimulate progress. For an amateur lifter, at least two workouts a week will suffice. As long as you keep showing up to training, the volume of work you will accumulate will allow you to succeed. It is also best to avoid breaks that last more than two days between training sessions.

Besides the actual training sets for kettlebell sport, a kettlebell athlete also needs to devote time to their general physical preparation (GPP), cardio-respiratory fitness, and flexibility (stretching). These other three components are performed as often as the main kettlebell sets (thrice a week) and can be done on the same day or on separate days as time and schedule allows (ex. KB + GPP on Monday, Cardio on Tuesday). The only exception is the flexibility component which should always be performed after the workout to accelerate recovery for the next session. You can also split the components into a morning and evening session (ex. KB + GPP in the morning, cardio in the evening).

Training schedule variations		Mo	Tu	We	Th	Fr	Sa	Su	Mo	Tu	We	Th	Fr	Sa	Su
I	a	KB	GPP, cardio	KB	GPP, cardio	KB	GPP, cardio		KB	GPP, cardio	KB	GPP, cardio	KB	GPP, cardio	
	b		KB	GPP, cardio	KB	GPP, cardio	KB	GPP, cardio		KB	GPP, cardio	KB	GPP, cardio	KB	GPP, cardio
II		KB	GPP, cardio	KB	GPP, cardio	KB	GPP, cardio	KB	GPP, cardio	KB	GPP, cardio	KB	GPP, cardio	KB	

Fig. 11. Weekly training schedule (+GPP and Cardio)

Tactical Planning for Long Cycle and Jerk

Tactical planning refers to specific programming within one training cycle, working backwards from your target competition date. Advanced athletes (males who have done a competition set with at least 20kg and females who have competed with 12kg) should take between 10-12 weeks to prepare for their target competition. Below is a sample tactical plan for an advanced athlete who plans to compete in either Long Cycle or Jerk with 32kg and has 12 weeks to prepare.

As a general rule, male/female professional lifters who regularly compete with 32kg/24kg should start their preparation with 16-20kg/8-12kg. Amateurs who compete with 24kg/16kg should begin with 16kg/8kg. Beginners who are starting out with 16kg/8kg should use 12kg/6kg.

It should also be noted that if you are going to perform an 8 minute test set with your competition weight, it should be scheduled no less than 3 weeks before the competition date. A 7 minute test set should be scheduled no less than 2 weeks prior to the competition. It usually takes 3-5 weeks of training on the competition weights to get ready for these test sets.

You can perform at least one 10 minute sets with lighter bells during the early half of the training cycle. Most of your time should be spent building up to the competition weights using lighter bells of increasing weight in no more than 2kg increments.

Below is a ready-to-implement example of a beginner Long Cycle or Jerk microcycle which uses all of the training methods discussed in the previous section. Take note that the third workout at the end of each week alternates between a Competition Method set

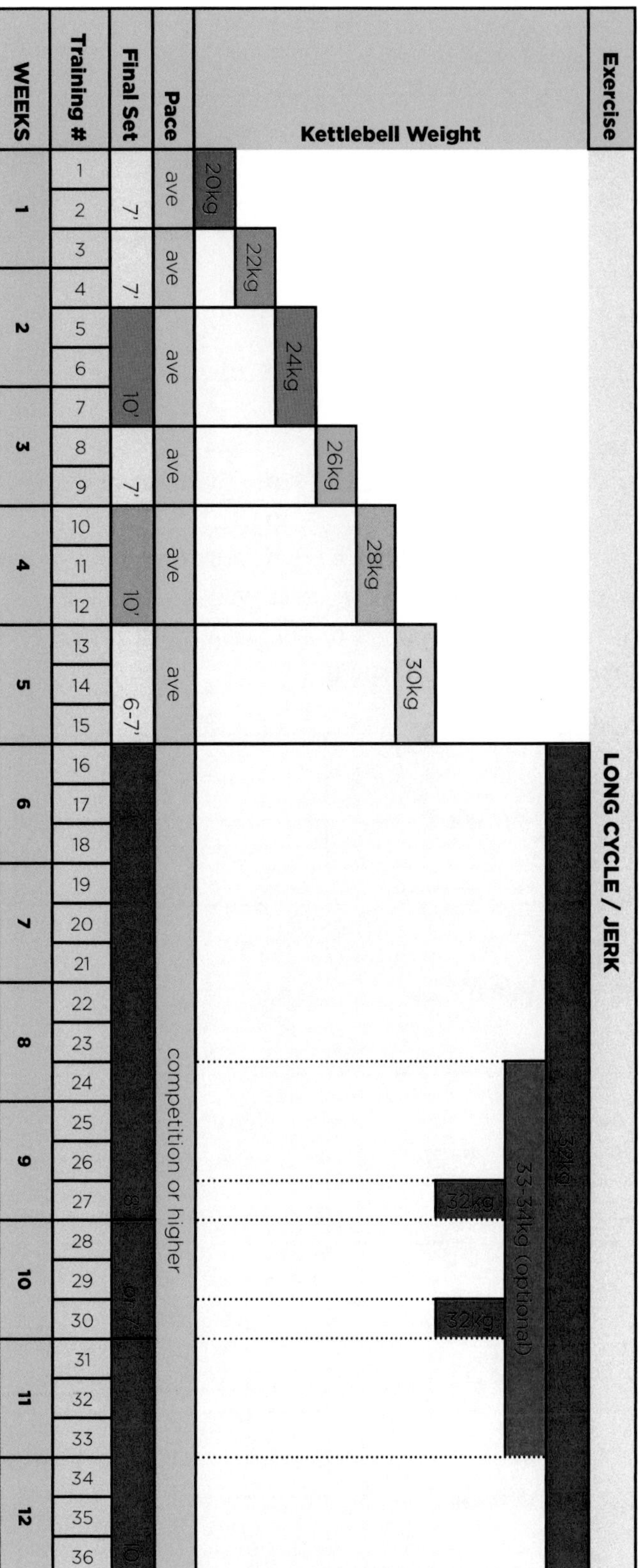

Fig. 12. Advanced Jerk/LC tactical plan

Long Cycle and Jerk Microcycle Estimate Structure

(one week long)

KB Workout # 1 short rest	KB Workout # 2 extended rest	KB Workout # 3 extended rest
Interval method Pyramid method Ladders method	Repetitive method Time pyramid method Ladders method	Competition method Flat method Variable method

Fig. 13. Jerk/LC microcycle structure

and an Interval/Repetitive/Time Pyramid and Ladder set every two weeks. As a general rule, long sets can be spaced out one week apart.

For people who have never done a 10 minute set before, the best strategy will be to start with Long Cycle using the lightest weights possible (12-16kg for males, 6-8kg for females). The goal at the end of this cycle is to complete a 10 minute set with decent technique, regardless of how many repetitions are performed.

Week 1	1min x 5 sets	2min x 3 sets	1min, 2min, 3min, 1min
	2min rest between sets	2-3min rest between sets	2min, 3min, 2min rest between sets
Week 2	1min x 7 sets	3min x 2 sets	**5min**
	1min rest between sets	3-5min rest between sets	
Week 3	2min x 4 sets	4min, 3min 2min, 1min	**7min TEST**
	2min rest between sets	4min, 3min, 2min, rest between sets	
Week 4	1min x 10 sets	3min x 3 sets	2min, 4min, 2min
	1min rest between sets	4-5min rest between sets	4min rest between sets
Week 5	3min, 2min, 1min	1min, 2min, 1min	**10min TEST**
	3min, 2min rest between sets	2min rest between sets	

Fig. 14. Beginner Jerk/LC tactical plan

On the way to the 10 minute set, there are two main test sets (5 minutes and 7 minutes) that need to be cleared. If the athlete fails to complete the 5 minute test, they will have to repeat workouts from the same week and redo the test at the end. Similarly, failure on the 7 minute test requires a repeat of the workouts from the same week. If the athlete fails on the main 10 minute set, they cannot move to a heavier bell during the next training cycle. The best plan is to reset to lighter weights and redo the 5 week preparation for that kettlebell weight. The entire process repeats until the 10 minute set is completed. If the athlete completes the set and performs more than 70 repetitions, only then can they increase the kettlebell weight by 2kg. If a male lifter successfully completes a 10 minute set with 20kg (female with 12kg), then they can move to a full sized training cycle of 10-12 weeks.

Progressive overload is achieved by gradually increasing the quantity and quality of performed work. You can track parameters such as:

Total duration of work
Length of rest periods
Lifting pace (repetitions per minute)
Weight of kettlebells
Number of exercises per training
Number of sets per training

There should be an emphasis on avoiding unilateral loading during a weekly or monthly cycle. The training process should be dynamic, interesting, and exciting. You should use all the training methods available to avoid staleness and getting stuck in just one particular method. It should be your goal to achieve a balanced development of multiple abilities including proficiency in lifting technique, agility, endurance, strength, strength-endurance, etc.

For an advanced lifter with stable technique and is looking to achieve a specific result at a target pace, the following table will serve as a useful guide for the main workouts that need to be completed. The closer the athlete can match the prescribed pace, the higher the chance for success on the test set.

> ***"Consistency is the key. Each workout skipped and each minute failed will decrease your chances to get a great result."***

TABLE A (aiming for 70 reps)

	minutes	1	2	3	4	5	6	7	8	9	10	reps total
Training #1 Variable method (50%)	a week before training #2	8	9	8	9	8						**42**
Training #2 Interval or Repetitive method	a week before training #3	9	8	9	rest	rest	rest	rest	rest			**26**
		9	9	9	rest	rest	rest	rest	rest			**27**
		9	8	9								**26**
Training #3a Flat method (70%)	2 weeks before competition	8	8	8	8	8	8	8				**56**
Training #3b Variable method (80%)	3 weeks before competition	7	8	7	8	7	8	7	8			**60**
Training #4 Interval method	next week after training #3	10	rest	10	rest	10	rest	10	rest	10	rest	**100**
		10	rest	10	rest	10	rest	10	rest	10		
COMPETITION		**7**	**7**	**7**	**7**	**7**	**7**	**7**	**7**	**7**	**7**	**70**

TABLE B (aiming for 80-85 reps)

	minutes	1	2	3	4	5	6	7	8	9	10	reps total
Training #1 Flat method (50%)	a week before training #2	10	10	10	10	10						**50**
Training #2 Interval or Repetitive method	a week before training #3	12	11	12	rest	rest	rest	rest	rest			**35**
		11	12	11	rest	rest	rest	rest	rest			**34**
		12	11	12								**35**
Training #3a Flat method (70%)	2 weeks before competitions	9	9	9	9	9	9	9				**63**
Training #3b Variable method (80%)	3 weeks before competitions	8	9	8	9	8	9	8	9			**68**
Training #4 Interval method	next week after training #3	11	rest	12	rest	11	rest	12	rest	11	rest	**115**
		11	rest	12	rest	11	rest	12	rest	12		
80COMPETITION		**8**	**8**	**8**	**8**	**8**	**8**	**8**	**8**	**8**	**8**	**80**

TABLE C (aiming for 90-95 reps)

	minutes	1	2	3	4	5	6	7	8	9	10	reps total
Training #1 Variable method (50%)	a week before training #2	11	11	12	11	12						**57**
Training #2 Interval method	a week before training #3	13	rest	13	rest	13	rest	13	rest	13	rest	**130**
		13	rest	13	rest	13	rest	13	rest	13		
Training #3 Repetitive method	a week before training #4	10	10	10	10	10	from 7 to 10-minute rest					**50**
		9	10	9	10	9	from 7 to 10-minute rest					**47**
		10	10	10	10	10						**50**
Training #4a Flat method (70%)	2 weeks before competition	10	10	10	10	10	10	10				**70**
Training #4b Variable method (80%)	3 weeks before competition	10	9	10	9	10	9	10	9			**76**
COMPETITION		**9**	**9**	**9**	**9**	**9**	**9**	**9**	**9**	**9**	**9**	**90**

TABLE D (aiming for 95-100 reps)

	minutes	1	2	3	4	5	6	7	8	9	10	reps total
Training #1 Flat method (50%)	a week before training #2	12	12	12	12	13						**61**
Training #2 Interval	a week before training #3	14	rest	14	rest	14	rest	14	rest	14	rest	**140**
		14	rest	14	rest	14	rest	14	rest	14		
Training #3 Repetitive method	a week before training #4	10	10	10	10	11	from 7 to 10-minute rest					**51**
		10	10	10	10	12	from 7 to 10-minute rest					**52**
		10	10	10	10	13						**53**
Training #4a Flat method (70%)	2 weeks before competition	11	11	11	11	11	11	11				**77**
Training #4a Flat method (80%)	3 weeks before competition	11	10	11	10	11	10	11	10			**84**
COMPETITION		**10**	**10**	**10**	**10**	**10**	**10**	**10**	**10**	**10**	**10**	**100**

Fig. 15. Advanced Jerk/LC pacing table

A great example that exemplifies the usefulness of this table is my preparation for the 2014 World Championships. Each training cycle has its own personality which reflects the environment that the athlete is currently in. My preparation was relatively short (only 7.5 weeks) which included an exhibition performance of a 10 minute Long Cycle with 28kg in Japan during the first week and a half of the cycle. This was a much more favorable scenario compared to having it in the middle of the cycle because it would not interfere with my training when I would already be working with 32kg.

However, the most interesting part about this particular training cycle was that Sergey Rachinsky, my coach at the time, surprised me with an unexpected modification to the 8 minute pre-competition test 2 weeks before the competition. Since our target for the world championships was 90 repetitions (an average of 9 repetitions per minute), my calculated pace for the 8 minute test according to the table was 10-11 repetitions per minute. I was cruising along during the set, until I realized in the final minute that Sergey's intention all along was to make me hit 90 repetitions in 8 minutes*! He saw that I was in great shape at that point so he decided to push for this result.

Overall I felt great and very much ready to give a strong performance at the World Championships. I had a lot of confidence heading into the competition and I was even able to hit pace 10 on the first and third minute of my set. My official result was 91 repetitions (with 1 no count for a repetition done after the time ran out)**. This was my best result in any IUKL competition then and since, and it was enough to secure the gold medal as well as establish a new world record in my weight class.

Fig. 16. 2014 World Championship diploma

---

* 8 minute test set (November 7 2014 - St. Petersburg, Russia): https://youtu.be/dAOU7rFFLXY

** IUKL World Championships 2014 (November 22 2014 - Hamburg, Germany): https://youtu.be/B9PCIHi35F0

MESOCYCLE	MICROCYCLES	Training Method	day	LONG CYCLE 2 x 32kg 2014 WORLD CHAMPIONSHIP TRAINING CYCLE			
				Long Cycle / Cleans			
				KB Weight	kind of work	given pace	completed
		OCTOBER 2014					
CHECK-PREPARATORY mesocycle	**Recovery**	Competing	2	**LC 24kg**	**3'**	**16-18rpm**	**16, 18, 19 (total 53r)**
			3				
		Interval	4	LC 26kg	3' x 2 sets (3' rest)	10rpm	10, 10, 10 / 10, 11, 12
	Refining		5				
		Interval	6	LC 26kg	4', 3' (4' rest)	10rpm	10, 10, 10, 10 / 10, 11, 12
			7				
		Interval ladder UP	8	LC 32kg	1', 2', 3' (2' rest)	10rpm	10 / 10, 10 / 10, 10, 13
			9	**Flight to Japan**			
	COMPETING		**10**	LC 28kg	10'	10rpm	**10, 10, 10, 10, 10, 10, 10, 10, 11, 13 (total 104 reps)**
			11	**OKCI Japan Championship**			
	Draw-in	Interval-Variable	12	LC 28kg, 30kg	4', 2' (4' rest)	11rpm	11, 11, 11, 12 / 11, 13
			13				
		Interval-Variable	14	LC 28kg, 30kg	5', 3' (5' rest)	11rpm	11, 11, 11, 11, 12 / 11, 11, 12
			15	Flight to Russia			
			16				
		Interval	17	LC 28kg	3', 4' (3' rest)	11rpm	11, 11, 11 / 11, 11, 11, 12
	COMPETING		**18**	**1HLC, 16kg (one KB)**	**60'**	**10rpm**	**total 600 reps**
			19	ONLINE by Jason Dolby			
BASE mesocycle	**Laborious #1**	Flat	**20**	**LC 30kg**	**5'**	**11rpm**	**11, 11, 11, 11, 13 (total 57r)**
			21				
		Interval-Variable	22	LC 30kg, 32kg	4, 3' (4' rest)	11rpm	11, 11, 11, 11, / 11, 11, 12
			23				
		Interval	24	LC 32kg	3' x 3 (3' rest)	11rpm	11, 11, 11 / 11, 11, 11 / 11, 11, 11
			25				
			26				

Fig. 17. 2014 World Championship training cycle

Mesocycle	Phase	Type	Day	Exercise	Duration	Pace	Result
BASE mesocycle (continuation)	Laborious #2	Competing	**27**	**LC 32KG**	**6'**	**11rpm**	11, 11, 11, 11, 11, 12 **(total 67reps)**
			28				
		Interval-Variable	29	LC 33kg, 34kg	4', 3' (4' rest)	11rpm	11, 11, 11, 11 / 11, 11, 12
			30				
		Flat	**31**	**LC 34kg**	**6'**	**9-10rpm**	10, 10, 10, 10, 10, 11 **(total 61 reps)**
		NOVEMBER 2014					
			1				
			2				
	Laborious #3	Interval-Variable	3	LC 32kg, 33kg **OA Cleans 32kg**	3', 2' (3' rest) **8' Right first**	11rpm **20rpm**	11, 11, 11 / 11, 12 **total 160rp**
			4				
		Interval	5	LC 34kg **OA Cleans 32kg**	1' x 7 sets (1' rest) **10' Left first**	12rpm **20rpm**	12 / 12 / 12 / 12 / 12 / 12 / 12 **total 200rp**
			6				
		Competing	7	**LC 32kg**	**8'**	**11rpm**	11, 11, 10, 10, 10, 10, 10, 11, 7 **(total 90r 8'35")**
PRE-COMPETITION mesocycle			8				
			9				
	Refining	Repetitive	10	LC 32kg **OA Cleans 32kg**	3' x 2 sets (4' rest) **L120+R120**	11rpm	11, 11, 11 / 11, 11, 12 **in 12'10"**
			11				
		Flat	12	**LC 34kg** **OA Cleans 32kg**	**4'** **14' Right first**	**10rpm** **20rpm**	**10, 10, 10, 12** **(total 42rp)** **total 288rp**
			13				
		Competing	**14**	**LC 32kg** **OA Cleans 32kg**	**3'** **L160+R160**	**15rpm**	**15, 15, 15+1** **(total 46r 3'03")** **in 20'**
			15		RELAY test		
			16				
	Recovery	Interval	17	LC 33kg **OA Cleans 32kg**	2' x 3 (2' rest) **16' Left first**	11rpm **20rpm**	11, 11 / 11, 11 / 11, 11 **total 320rp**
			18				
			19				
		Repetitive	20	LC 32kg	1', 1'30", 1'30" (3' rest)	10rpm	10 / 10, 5 / 10, 5
			21				
		Competing	**22**	LC 32kg	10'	10rpm	**10, 9, 10, 9, 9, 9,** **9, 8, 9, 9+1** **(total 92r,** **1 no count)**
			23	**IUKL World Championship, Hamburg, Germany**			

Fig. 17. 2014 World Championship training cycle

Tactical Planning for Snatch

Programming for Snatch is simpler and more straightforward compared to Long Cycle and Jerk. This discipline doesn't require as much strength but demands a higher level of precision in technique, speed of movement, and endurance. It only requires one kettlebell and you can switch hands once at any moment during the competition set. Such conditions make the Snatch suitable for training sets lasting longer than 10 minutes of work, especially when using lighter weights. The Competition method and its variations is the favored approach to Snatch training because it develops muscle memory, which is crucial to establishing stable technique that can last for hundreds of repetitions. I also consider Snatch to be the most cyclical type of exercise compared to Long Cycle and Jerk.

Advanced athletes (males who have done a competition set with at least 20kg and females who have competed with 12kg) should take between 10-12 weeks to prepare for their target competition. Below is a sample tactical plan for an athlete who plans to compete in Snatch with 32kg and has 12 weeks to prepare.

As a general rule, male/female professional lifters who regularly compete with 32kg/24kg should start their preparation with 16kg/8kg. Amateurs who compete with 24kg/16kg should begin with 12-16kg/6-8kg. Beginners who are starting out with 16kg/8kg should use 8-12kg/4-6kg.

The most important test leading up to a competition set is the 8 minute test set with your competition weight and it should be completed 1 week before the competition date. It is also possible to perform this test set with a rest period in between arms depending on the athlete's preparation (4 minutes left hand, 4-8 minutes rest, 4 minutes right hand.) It usually takes 2-4 weeks of training to get ready for a 10 minute set on the same weight and even less when using lighter weights. When building up to competition weights, you should

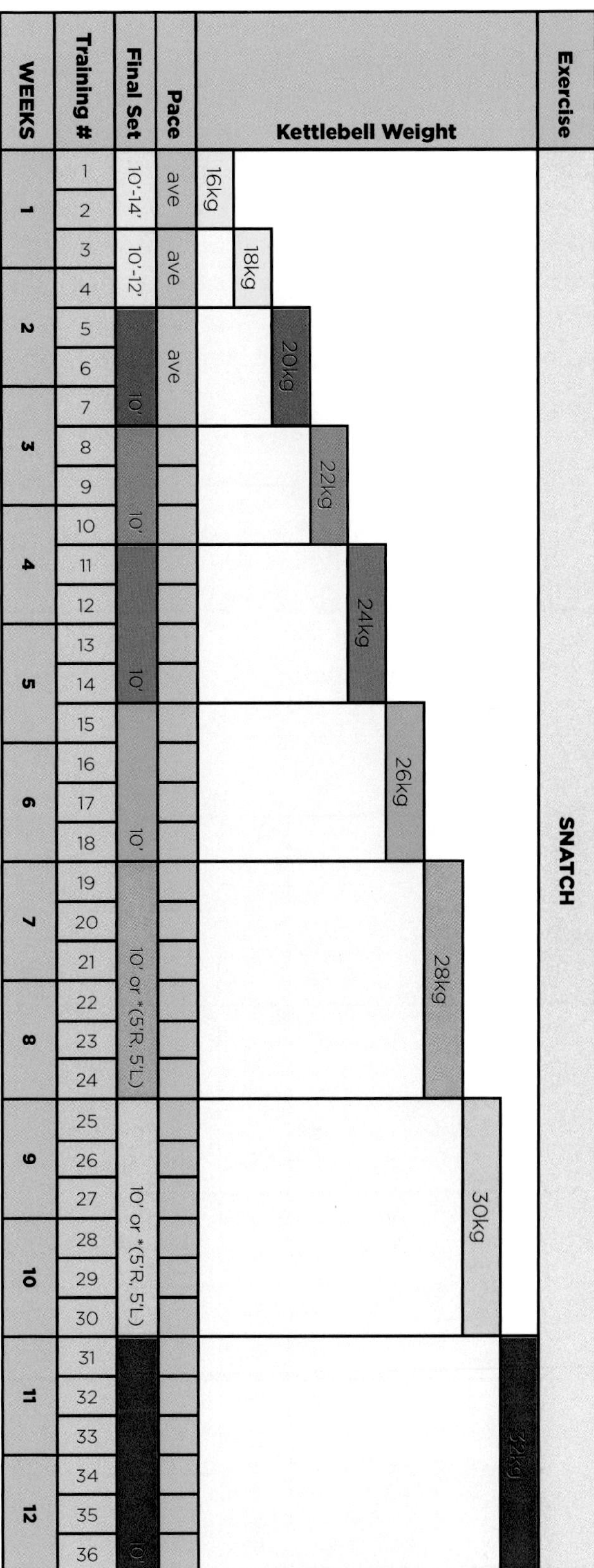

WEEKS	Training #	Final Set	Pace	Kettlebell Weight	Exercise
1	1	10'-14'	ave	16kg	SNATCH
	2				
	3	10'-12'	ave	18kg	
2	4				
	5	10'	ave	20kg	
	6				
3	7				
	8	10'		22kg	
	9				
4	10				
	11	10'		24kg	
	12				
5	13				
	14				
	15	10'		26kg	
6	16				
	17				
	18				
7	19	10' or *(5'R, 5'L)		28kg	
	20				
	21				
8	22				
	23				
	24				
9	25	10' or *(5'R, 5'L)		30kg	
	26				
	27				
10	28				
	29				
	30				
11	31	10'		32kg	
	32				
	33				
12	34				
	35				
	36				

Fig. 18. Advanced Snatch tactical plan

always perform a 10 minute test set every 2-4 weeks progressing from lighter to heavier bells using no more than 2kg increments.

Below is a ready-to-implement example of a beginner Snatch microcycle which uses all of the training methods discussed in the previous section. Advanced athletes can train exclusively by alternating the Interval and Competition methods, leaving out the Repetitive method. Take note that the third workout at the end of each week alternates between a Competition Method set and an Interval/Repetitive/Time Pyramid and Ladder set every two weeks. As an additional detail, KB workout #1 can be completely omitted from the training process of advanced athletes. Their microcycle would consist of only two workout types (#2 and #3) alternating as pairs over four days. The first workout would be an Interval/Repetitive/Time Pyramid and Ladder set followed by a Competition/Flat/Variable set.

Snatch Microcycle Estimate Structure

(one week long)

KB Workout # 1 short rest	KB Workout # 2 extended rest	KB Workout # 3 extended rest
Interval method Pyramid method Ladders method	Repetitive method Time pyramid method Ladders method	Competition method Flat method Variable method

Fig. 19. Snatch microcycle structure

Week 1	LEFT FIRST	2min x 4 sets 2min rest between sets	RIGHT FIRST	4min x 2 sets 4min rest between sets	LEFT FIRST	**6min**
Week 2	RIGHT FRIST	2min x 5 sets 2min rest between sets	LEFT FIRST	4min x 3 sets 4min rest between sets		**4min** RIGHT, **4min** LEFT 4-8min rest between sets
Week 3	LEFT FIRST	4min x 2 sets 2-4min rest between sets	RIGHT FIRST	6min x 2 sets 6-8min rest between sets	LEFT FIRST	**8min TEST**
Week 4	RIGHT FIRST	4min x 2 sets 4min rest between sets	LEFT FIRST	2min x 4 sets 2min rest between sets		**10min TEST**

Fig. 20. Beginner Snatch tactical plan

For people who are new to Snatch, the best strategy will be to complete a 4 week training cycle using the lightest weight possible (8-12kg for males, 4-8kg for females). The same weight should be used throughout the entire cycle. The goal is to complete a 10 minute set with decent technique, regardless of how many repetitions are performed.

On the way to the 10 minute set, there are three main test sets (6 minutes, 4+4 minutes and 8 minutes) that need to be cleared. The athlete is not allowed to move forward to the next week if they are unable to complete the test at the end of the week. If the athlete fails to complete the 6 minute test, they will have to repeat workouts from the same week and redo the test at the end. If the athlete fails on the main 10 minute set, they cannot move to a heavier bell during the next training cycle. The best plan is to reset to lighter weights and redo the 4 week preparation for that kettlebell weight. The entire process repeats until the 10 minute set is completed. If the athlete completes the set and performs more than 140 repetitions, only then can they increase the kettlebell weight by 2kg.

A fundamental rule of this methodology is that each training method and its variations should be viewed as independent instruments for developing specific training qualities at a specific moment of the training cycle. Each mesocycle and microcycle should have a purpose. Each workout should be built on the principles of gradual increase in workload, which are determined by the following parameters:

Total duration of work
Length of rest periods
Lifting pace (repetitions per minute)
Weight of kettlebells
Number of exercises per training
Number of sets per training

Staleness in training should be avoided as much as possible. The process should be kept dynamic and exciting. It is therefore important to avoid unilateral loading during the week and month. You should use and combine all of the tools at your disposal and not get stuck in only one type of training. A well-rounded approach will yield an optimal balance of all the necessary training qualities which include technique, agility, endurance, strength, and strength-endurance. Below is an example of the various training methods used in Snatch.

TRAINING METHOD	SET DURATION*									
	2min	4min	6min	8min	10min	12min	14min	16min	18min	20min
Interval method	x 3-5 sets	x 2-4 sets	x 2 sets							
Repetitive method	x 3-5 sets	x 2-4 sets	x 2-3 sets							
Flat method			x 1 set	x 1 set	x 1 set	x 1 set	x 1 set	x 1 set	x 1 set	x 1 set
Variable method			x 1 set	x 1 set	x 1 set	x 1 set	x 1 set	x 1 set	x 1 set	x 1 set
Competing method (kettlebell of competition weight)			x 1 set	x 1 set	x 1 set	x 1 set				

Fig. 21. Snatch training methods

It's possible to take a rest between arms during the Competing method. The rest intervals between work sets is similar to the rest duration used in the Interval and Repetitive methods. The hand switch during the working set should be performed approximately at the halfway mark of the set duration (ex. switch at 5 minutes during a 10 minute set). The pace for all Snatch training sessions should be 90-110% of your target competition pace.

Tactical Planning for Biathlon

Biathlon in kettlebell sport refers to performing the Jerk and Snatch during competition with at least 30 minutes of rest in between. To prepare for such a demanding performance, I recommend doing both the Jerk and Snatch training sets in the same workout.

The Jerk is considered to be more of a strength exercise and requires a longer preparation (up to 8 weeks) to work up to competition weights. On the other hand, the Snatch is more of a speed and endurance exercise and peaking for this discipline happens within a very short time frame (2-7 days).

As such, both exercises complement each other quite well because when the Jerk training sets are at their maximum intensity, the Snatch workouts are still relatively light. Conversely, when the Snatch workouts become more intense, the Jerk workouts are easier with a lower volume of work. Below is an example tactical plan for Biathlon.

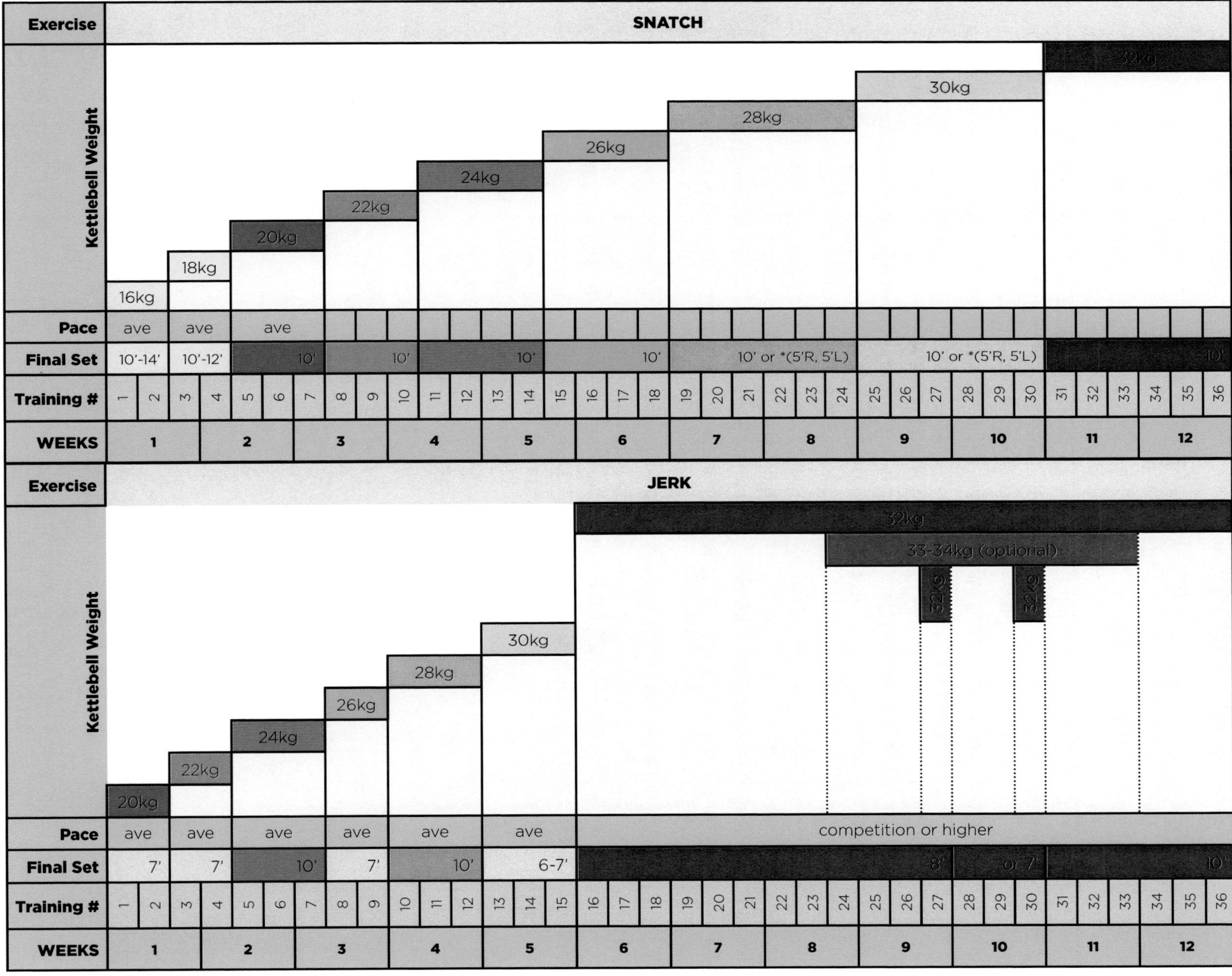

Exercise	WEEKS	Training #	Final Set	Pace	Kettlebell Weight
SNATCH	1	1–2	10'-14'	ave	16kg
	2	3–4	10'-12'	ave	18kg
	2–3	5–7	10'	ave	20kg
	3–4	8–10	10'		22kg
	4–5	11–14	10'		24kg
	5–6	15–18	10'		26kg
	7–8	19–24	10' or *(5'R, 5'L)		28kg
	9–10	25–30	10' or *(5'R, 5'L)		30kg
	11–12	31–36	10'		32kg

Exercise	WEEKS	Training #	Final Set	Pace	Kettlebell Weight
JERK	1	1–2	7'	ave	20kg
	2	3–4	7'	ave	22kg
	2–3	5–7	10'	ave	24kg
	3	8–9	7'	ave	26kg
	4	10–12	10'	ave	28kg
	5	13–15	6-7'	ave	30kg
	6–8	16–23	8'	competition or higher	32kg
	8–9	24–27	8'	competition or higher	32kg; 33-34kg (optional); 32kg (training 27)
	10	28–30	or 7'	competition or higher	32kg; 33-34kg (optional); 32kg (training 30)
	11	31–33	10'	competition or higher	32kg; 33-34kg (optional)
	12	34–36	10'	competition or higher	32kg

Fig. 22. Advanced Biathlon tactical plan

Tactical Planning for Triathlon

Triathlon in kettlebell sport refers to performing the Long Cycle, Jerk, and Snatch during competition with at least 30 minutes of rest in between. Preparation for these three events revolves mainly around training the Jerk and Snatch (Biathlon training) with the occasional short set of Cleans or Long Cycle performed once a week or once every two weeks.

The reason for this is that the Jerk and Snatch positively benefit the Long Cycle without having to train it specifically. As I previously mentioned, the Long Cycle already contains the Jerk and the Clean portion of the exercise is pretty much a shorter amplitude of the Snatch movement and is performed with two bells instead of one. This is why experienced Biathlon specialists can easily jump into a Long Cycle competition and perform about 80-90% of their best Long Cycle result.

Conversely, I've also noticed that Long Cycle specialists have no trouble competing in Snatch while in the middle of their Long Cycle training. It is typical for them to expect results of about 80-90% of their best Snatch results. However, even if the Long Cycle benefits the Snatch because of the power required to clean two bells, the two exercises should not be trained together because it is easy to overwork the forearm and hand muscles. The skin on the palms also becomes an issue once a large volume of gripping and regripping is introduced.

In relation to the Jerk, the Long Cycle disrupts the specific skill of being able to rest in the Rack Position. The fact that you can Clean the bells after every repetition allows the athlete to get away with a less than optimal Rack Position. The whole dynamic of the Long Cycle doesn't feel as crisp and fast as the Jerk and indeed, jumping into Biathlon after spending time in the Long Cycle requires a period of adjustment. Since the pace of the Jerk is much faster than in Long Cycle, the overall movement initially feels less precise and this leads to fatigue much sooner. However, as the Biathlon training cycle progresses, the proper rhythm of the Jerk becomes much more established and lifting becomes more comfortable.

A perfect example of this was during my Biathlon preparation in June 2019. I had 8 weeks to prepare for Biathlon with 24kg so I started light with 16kg on both the Jerk and Snatch. The unusual circumstance during this cycle was that I had to fly to Manila 6 weeks into my Biathlon program to compete in Long Cycle. I knew that my preparation in Jerk would cover a large part of the Long Cycle technique and that I only had to make minor adjustments to my standard Biathlon training process to accommodate this fact.

Specifically, the main modification was that I scheduled my 24kg Snatch gym test 10 days before the Long Cycle competition because I knew that training Snatch and Cleans together would easily overwork my grip and test the durability of the skin on my palms. Afterwards, I only did Jerk and Cleans for the next 3 training sessions and I only did a complete Long Cycle session 2 days before competition. As it turned out I was able to get 131 repetitions which was higher than my target of between 120-130 repetitions.[*] More importantly, I felt like my result was only 5-10% less of what I might get if I were on a specialized Long Cycle preparation.

The following week, with only 2 weeks left until my main Biathlon competition, I went back to training Jerk and Snatch together again. That one week of doing only Cleans and Long Cycle did not undo any of my preparation for Snatch and I was actually able to beat my gym test result by 1 repetition. In the end, I was very satisfied with the results I got which were 204 repetitions in Jerk and 262 repetitions in Snatch for a total Biathlon score of 335 points[**].

---

* IKO Asian Championships (June 12, 2019 - Manila, Philippines: https://youtu.be/7OcY-vaF8pg

** Crazy Monkey USA Nationals (June 29, 2019 - Seattle, USA): https://youtu.be/5z4uolrACho

Considering the professional level I had already achieved in kettlebell sport, the 24kg bells did not exhaust me and I still had plenty of energy to continue up to 32kg. I had 7 weeks until my next competition and the timing for both my Jerk and Snatch test sets couldn't have been more perfect. For Jerk, I had 4 weeks to prepare for my 7 minute test on my competition weight of 32kg and an additional 2 weeks of final preparation. For Snatch, I started with 26kg and increased the weight by 2kg. For the 26kg and 28kg bells, I spent 1 week on each weight. For the 30kg and 32kg bells I spent 2 weeks on each. weight. This was more than enough time to perform my 10 minute gym tests on every single weight increment. The end result was that I was able to score my highest results in Jerk (145 repetitions), Snatch (203 repetitions), and Biathlon total (246.5 points) in competition.*

			4	LC 32kg	10'	9rpm	**9, 9, 8, 8, 7, 7, 7, 7,9, 12 (total 83r)**	
			5	**Great Plains Kettlebell Sport Competition**				
MESOCYCLE	**MICROCYCLES**			**KETTLEBELL BIATHLON 2 x 32kg TRAINING CYCLE NorCal KB Sport Open 2019**				
				Jerk				
			day	KB Weight	kind of work	given pace	completed	
		Training Method		**May 2019**				
DRAW-IN meocycle	**Darw-in # 1**	Interval	6	Jerk 18kg	2' x 3 sets (2' rest)	20rpm	19, 20 / 20, 22 / 22, 24	
			7	Flight from Wichita, KS to SF, CA				
			8					
		Competing - Variable	**9**	**Jerk 18kg**	**4'**	**20rpm**	**19, 20, 20, 22 (total 82rp)**	**1**
			10					
		Interval	11	Jerk 20kg	1' x 5 sets (1' rest)	20-24rpm	22 / 24 / 25 / 25 / 27	
			12					
	Draw-in # 2		13					
		Repetitive	14	Jerk 20kg	3' x 3 (5' rest)	20-24rpm	19, 20, 21 / 21, 22, 23 / 22, 24, 27	
			15					
		Competing - Variable	**16**	**Jerk 20kg**	**5'**	**20-24rpm**	**21, 22, 22, 24, 27 (total 116rp)**	**2**
			17					
		Interval	18	Jerk 24kg	1' x 6 sets (1' rest)	20-24rpm	20 / 22 / 23 / 23 / 23 / 26	
			19					
BASE mesocycle	**Laborious # 1**		20					
		Time Pyramid - Repetitive	21	Jerk 24kg	1', 2', 3', 1' (2', 3', 2' rest)	20-24rpm	22 / 22, 22 / 22, 22, 23 / 25	
			22					**3**
		Interval	23	Jerk 24kg	2' x 4 (2' rest)	20-24rpm	22, 22 / 22, 23 / 22, 24 / 23, 26	
			24					

* North California Open KB Sport Competition (August 17, 2019 - California, USA): https://youtu.be/aYwFILIhJWg

Mesocycle	Phase	Type	Day	Exercise	Time	Pace	Reps	Week
BASE mesocycle		Competing - Flat	**25**	**Jerk 24kg**	**4'**	**20-24rpm**	**22, 22, 22, 26 (total 92rp)**	
			26					
	Laborious # 2	Interval	27	Jerk 24kg	1' x 7 (1' rest)	22-25rpm	24 / 24 / 25 / 25 / 26 / 26 / 28	4
			28					
		Repetitive	29	Jerk 24kg	3' x 2 sets (5' rest)	20-24rpm	22, 22, 24 / 22, 23, 26	
			30					
		Competing - Flat	**31**	**Jerk 24kg**	**5'**	**20-24rpm**	**22, 22, 22, 24, 27 (total 117rp)**	
			June 2019					
			1					
			2					
	Laborious # 3	Interval	3	Jerk 24kg	2' x 4 (2' rest)	20-24rpm	22, 22 / 22, 22 / 22, 23 / 23, 27	5
			4					
		Ladder DOWN - Interval	5	Jerk 24kg	4', 3', 2', 1' (4', 3', 2' rest)	22-24rpm	22, 22, 22, 24 / 22, 22, 24 / 23, 27 / 30	
			6					
		Competing - Flat	7	**Jerk 24kg**	**7'**	**22-24rpm**	**22, 22, 22, 22, 22, 22, 24 (total 156rp)**	
	Refining		8	Flight to Metro Manila, Philippines				
			9					
		Interval	10	LC 24kg	2' x 3 sets (2' rest)	12rpm	12, 12 / 12, 13 / 12, 15	6
			11					
		Competing	**12**	LC 24kg	10'	12-13rpm	**12, 12, 13, 13, 13, 13, 13, 14, 14, 15 (total 132rp)**	
PRE-COMPETITION mesocycle	Recovery		13	Asian Championship, Metro Manila, PH				
			15	L3 course				
			16	L3 course				
	Refining # 1		17	L3 course				7
		Interval	18	Jerk 24kg	2' x 3 sets (2' rest)	22rpm	22, 22 / 22, 23 / 23, 25	
			19	Flight from Metro Manila, PH to SF, CA				
			20					
		Ladder UP - Repetitive	21	Jerk 24kg	2', 4' (5' rest)	22rpm	22, 23 / 20, 21, 23, 24	
			22					
		Time Pyramid - Repetitive	23	Jerk 24kg	1', 2', 3', 2', 1' (2', 3', 2', 2' rest)	22rpm	22 / 22, 23 / 22, 22 24 / 22, 25 / 26	

Mesocycle	Microcycle	Training Method	day	KB Weight	kind of work	given pace	completed	
PRE-COMP cont	Refining # 2		24					8
		Interval	25	Jerk 24kg	3' x 2 (2' rest)	22rpm	22, 22, 24 / 22, 22, 23	
			26					
		Ladder DOWN - Interval	27	Jerk 24kg	3', 2', 1' (2' rest)	22rpm	22, 22, 22 / 22, 23	
			28					
		Competing	**29**	Jerk 24kg	10'		**20, 20, 20, 20, 20, 20, 20, 20, 21, 23 (total 204rp)**	
			30	US Nationals by Crazy Monkey USA & IKO KB World League				

Fig. 23.a. Biathlon (Jerk) and Long Cycle training Cycle

MESOCYCLE	MICROCYCLES	Training Method	day	KB Weight	kind of work	given pace	completed	
			4	Jerk 16kg DHS 12kg	10' 10'		**239rp 200rp**	
			5	**Snatch 32kg**	**5'**	**20rpm**	**R54+L56 total 110rp**	
				KETTLEBELL BIATHLON 2 x 32kg TRAINING CYCLE NorCal KB Sport Open 2019				
				Snatch				
				May 2019				
		Competing	**6**	Snatch 16kg	10' Right first		**Total 255rp**	
DRAW-IN mesocyce	Draw-in		7	Flight from Wichita, KS to SF, CA				
			8					
		Competing	**9**	**Snatch 18kg**	**6'**		**R71+L71 Total 142rp**	
			10					
		Competing	**11**	Snatch 18kg	10' Left first	22-25rpm	**L130+R134 Total 264r**	
			12					
	Refining # 1		13					
		Competing	**14**	**Snatch 20kg**	**6' Right first**	**22-25rpm**	**R71+L73 Total 144r**	
			15					
		Repetitive	16	**Snatch 20kg**	**4'L, 4'R (8' rest)**	**22-25rpm**	**R24, 24, 25, 27 / L24, 24, 25, 27**	
			17					
		Competitive	**18**	Snatch 20kg	10' Right first	22-25rpm	**R126+L130 Total 256rp**	
			19					
	Ref. # 2		20					
		Competing	**21**	**Snatch 22kg**	**6' Left first**	**22-25rpm**	**L75+R75 Total 150rp**	
			22					

DRAW-IN mesocycle (cont.)	Ref. # 2 cont	Repetitive	23	**Snatch 22kg**	**4'R, 4'L (8' rest)**	**22-25rpm**	**R100(4'04") / L100**	
			24					
		Competing	**25**	Snatch 22kg	10' Left first	22-25rpm	**L130+R133 Total 263rp**	
			26					
	Refining # 3	Competing	27	**Snatch 24kg**	**6' Right first**	**22-25rpm**	**R75+L75 Total 150rp**	
			28					
		Repetitive	29	**Snatch 24kg**	**4'L, 4'R (8' rest)**	**22-25rpm**	**L100 / R100**	
			30					
		Competing	**31**	Snatch 24kg	10' Right first	22-25rpm	**R130+L131 Total 261rp**	
		June 2019						
			1	Cleans 24kg	Cleans 2' (2' rest)		15, 20 Total 35rp	
			2					
			3	Cleans 24kg	Cleans 2' (2' rest)		15, 21 Total 36rp	
			4					
			5	Cleans 24kg	Cleans 2' (2' rest)		14, 16 Total 30rp	
			6					
			7					
			8	Flight to Metro Manila, Philippines				
			9					
			10					
			11					
			12					
			13					
			14	L3 course				
			15	L3 course				
			16	L3 course				
			17					
DRAW-IN mesocycle	Competing	Competing	**18**	Snatch 16kg	10' Right first	25rpm	**R132+L133 Total 256rp**	
			19	flight from Metro Manila, PH to SF, CA				
			20					
		Competing	**21**	Snatch 18kg	10' Left first	25rpm	**L131+R131 Total 262rp**	
			22					
		Competing	**23**	Snatch 20kg	10' Right first	25rpm	**R132+L132 Total 264rp**	

DRAW-IN mseo	Refining		24					
		Competing	**25**	**Snatch 24kg**	**6' Left first**	**25rpm**	**L72+R72**	
			26					
		Repetitive	27	**Snatch 24kg**	**4'R, 4'L (5' rest)**	**25rpm**	**R98+2 / L 98+2**	
			28	Drive to Everett, WA				
		Competing	**29**	Snatch 24kg	10' Right first	25-27rpm	**R160 (6'50")+L102 Total 262rp**	
			30	US Nationals by Crazy Monkey USA & IKO KB World League			BT score 335pts	

Fig. 23.b. Biathlon (Snatch) and Long Cycle training Cycle

		July 2019					
DRAW-IN mesocycle	Draw-in # 1		1				
		Interval	2	Jerk 28kg	1' x 5 sets (1' rest)	15-20rpm	17 / 19 / 20 / 21 / 24
			3				
		Interval	4	Jerk 28kg	2' x 3 sets (2' rest)	16-18rpm	16, 17 / 18, 19 / 20, 21
			5				
		Time Pyramid - Repetitive	6	Jerk 28kg	1', 2', 3', 2', 1' (2', 3', 2', 2' rest)	16-18rpm	18 / 18, 18 / 18, 18, 19 / 18, 21 / 26
			7				
	Drawi-in # 2		8				
		Competing - Variable	**9**	**Jerk 28kg**	**5'**	**16-18rpm**	**18, 18, 18, 20, 23 Total 97rp**
			10				
		Interval	11	Jerk 32kg	1' x 5 sets (1' rest)	15-20rpm	16 / 18 / 18 / 20 / 21
			12				
		Interval	13	Jerk 32kg	2' x 3 sets (2' rest)	15-18rpm	15, 16 / 16. 18 / 16, 20
			14				
BASE mesocycle	Laborious # 1		15				
		Time Pyramid - Repetitive	16	Jerk 32kg	1', 2', 3', 1' (2', 3', 2' rest)	15-18rpm	16 / 14, 16 / 15, 16, 18 / 23
			17				
		Repetitive	18	Jerk 32kg	3' x 2 sets (5' rest)	15-18rpm	15, 16, 16 / 16, 16, 17 / 16, 17, 20
			19				
		Competing - Flat	**20**	**Jerk 32kg**	**5'**	**15-18rpm**	**16, 16, 16, 16, 20 Total 84rp**
			21				
			22				

BASE mesocycle cont.	Laborious # 2	Interval	23	Jerk 32kg	1' x 7 sets (1' rest)	18-22rpm	19 / 20 / 20 / 20 / 21 / 22 / 22
			24				
		Ladder DOWN - Interval	25	Jerk 32kg	4', 3', 2', 1' (4', 3', 2' rest)	16-18rpm	16, 16, 16, 17 / 16, 16, 18 / 18, 19 / 23
			26				
		Competing - Flat	27	**Jerk 32kg**	**6'**	**16rpm**	**16, 16, 16, 16, 16, 20 Total 100rp**
			28				
	Laborious # 3		29				
		Interval	30	Jerk 32kg	2' x 5 sets (2' rest)	16-18rpm	16, 17 / 16, 16 / 16, 17 / 16, 18 / 18, 20
			31				
					August 2019		
		Repetitive	1	Jerk 32kg	4' x 3 sets (6' rest)	16rpm	16, 16, 16, 16 / 16, 16, 16, 17 / 16, 16, 16, 19
			2				
		Competing - Flat	3	**Jerk 32kg**	**7'**	**16rpm**	**16, 16, 16, 16, 16, 16, 17 Total 113rp**
PRE-COMPETITION mesocycle	Laborious # 4		4				
		Interval	5	Jerk 32kg	1' x 10 sets (1' rest)	20-22rpm	20 / 20 / 20 / 20 / 20 / 21 / 21 / 21 / 22 / 24
			6				
		Ladder UP - Interval	7	Jerk 32kg	1', 2', 3', 4' (1', 2', 3' rest)	16rpm	17 / 16, 17 / 16, 16, 17 / 16, 16, 16, 20
			8				
			9				
	Refining	Competing - Flat	10	**Jerk 32kg**	**4'**	**18rpm**	**18, 18, 18, 20 Total 74rp**
			11				
			12				
		Ladder DOWN - Interval	13	Jerk 32kg	3', 2', 1' (2' rest)	16rpm	16, 16, 18 / 16, 18 / 20
			14				
		Pyramid - Repetitive	15	Jerk 32kg	1', 2', 1' (2')	16rpm	16 / 16, 16 / 20
			16				
		Competing	17	Jerk 32kg	10'	15rpm	15, 15, 15, 15, 15, 14, 13, 13, 14, 16 Total 145rp
			18	**Northern California Open KB Sport Competition 2019**			

Fig. 24.a. Biathlon (jerk) and Long Cycle training cycle (2)

		9July 2019					
DRAW-IN mesocycle	Draw-in # 1		1				
		Interval	2	Snatch 26kg	4' x 2 sets (4' rest)	25rpm	R44+L44 / R 46+L46
			3		Right first		
		Competing	**4**	**Snatch 26kg**	**6' Left first**	**25rpm**	**L70+R70 Total 170rp**
			5				
		Repetitive	6	Snatch 26kg	4'L, 4'R (5' rest)	22-24rpm	R92 / L92
			7				
	Draw-in $ 2		8				
		Competing	**9**	Snatch 26kg	10' Left first	22-24rpm	**L120+R120 Total 240rp**
			10				
		Interval	11	Snatch 28kg	4' x 2 sets (4' rest)	22-24rpm	R43+L43 / R45+L45
			12		Right frist		
		Competing	**13**	Snatch 28kg	6' Left first	22-24rpm	**L65+R66 Total 131rp**
			14				
	Laborious # 1		15				
		Repetitive	16	Snatch 28kg	4'R, 4'L (5' rest)	22-24rpm	R92+L92
			17				
		Competiting	**18**	Snatch 28kg	10' Left first	22-24rpm	**L21, 23, 23, 24, 25 (117rp) + R21, 23, 24, 24, 24, 24 (117rp) Total 234rp**
			19				
		Interval	20	Snatch 30kg	4' x 2 sets (4' rest)	22-24rpm	R42+L42 / R44+L44
			21		Right first		
	Laborious # 2		22				
		Competing	23	**Snatch 30kg**	**6' Left first**	**22-24rpm**	**L65+R63 (+2) Total 128(+2)**
			24				
		Interval	25	Snatch 30kg	3' x 3 sets (3' rest)	22-24rpm	R32+L32 / R32+L33 / R33+L34
			26		Right first		
		Repetitive	27	Snatch 30kg	4'L, 4'R (6' rest)	22-24rpm	L21, 21, 21, 23 / R22, 21, 23, 23
			28				
	Lab. # 3		29				
		Repetitive	30	Snatch 30kg	6' x 2 sets (10' rest)	20-22rpm	R21, 21, 21 + L20, 21, 22 / R21, 22, 22 +L21,22,23
			31		Right first		

Mesocycle	Microcycle	Method	Day	Exercise	Duration	Pace	Result
BASE meso.	Laborious # 3				August 2019		
		Competing	1	Snatch 30kg	10' Left first	20-22rpm	**L107+R108 Total 215rp**
			2				
		Interval	3	Snatch 32kg	4' x 2 sets (4' rest)	20-22rpm	R42+L42 / R43+L44
PRE-COMPETITION mesocycle			4		Right first		
	Laborious # 4	Competing	**5**	**Snatch 32kg**	**6' Right first**	**20-22rpm**	**R63+L64 Total 127**
			6				
		Interval	7	Snatch 32kg	3' x 3 sets (3' rest)	20-22rpm	L31+R31 / L32+R32 / L34+R34
			8		Left first		
			9				
		Repetitive	10	Snatch 32kg	4'R, 4'L (8' rest)	20-22rpm	R88 / L90 (6' rest)
			11				
	Refining		12				
		Repetitive	13	Snatch 32kg	6' x 2 sets (10' rest)	20-22rpm	L63+R63 / L64+R64
			14		Left first		
		Interval	15	Snatch 32kg	4' x 2 sets (4' rest)	20-22rpm	R43+L43 / R45+R45
			16		Right first		
		Competition	17	Snatch 32kg	10' Left first	20-22rpm	**L21, 21, 21, 20, 21, 21 (104rp in 5'05") + R17,21, 21, 22, 18 (99rp), Total 203rp**
			18				BT score 246.5pts

Fig. 24.b. Biathlon (snatch) and Long Cycle training cycle (2)

Strategic and Tactical Planning Overview

A fundamental rule of my methodology is that each training method and its variations should be viewed as independent instruments for developing specific training qualities at a specific moment of the training cycle. Each mesocycle and microcycle should have a purpose. Each workout should be built on the principles of gradual increase in workload, which are determined by the following parameters: total duration of work, length of rest periods, lifting pace, weight of kettlebells, number of exercises per training, number of sets per training.

Staleness in training should be avoided as much as possible. The process should be kept dynamic and exciting. It is therefore important to avoid unilateral loading during the week and month. You should use and combine all of the tools at your disposal and not get stuck in only one type of training. A well-rounded approach will yield an optimal balance of all the necessary training qualities which include technique, agility, endurance, strength, and strength-endurance.

It is also important to remember that being a kettlebell sport athlete is like being an athlete in any other sport. The demands are very challenging and complex. Everything you do in your life matters and must be taken into account. As a matter of fact, the training you do for kettlebell sport is only one part of all the other activities you engage in. All the elements of your life should be in harmony. The better you can balance each element with all the others, the chances of succeeding in kettlebell sport increases. When we are looking for areas to improve in, we should pay as much attention to the overall quality of our life and work schedule as we do to our kettlebell training.

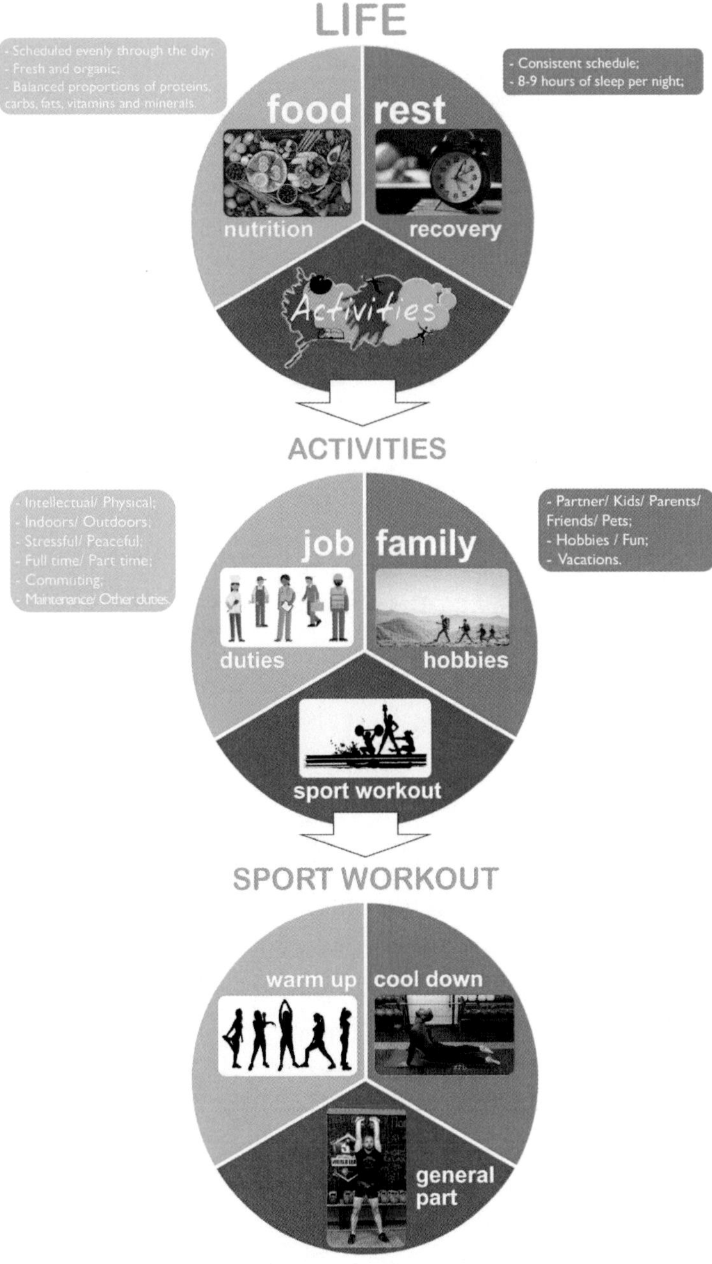

Fig. 25. Life, activities, and sport

Where to Begin

One of the best things about kettlebell sport is that you can practically start training at any age. It's much better to start younger, but there are numerous examples of older athletes who were able to show world class results after going through a few training cycles. Below is a sample strategic plan for a young, motivated, disciplined, and talented athlete who wants to begin their career in kettlebell sport.

During the first year, each training cycle with a specific weight lasts about 3-5 weeks and always ends with a 10 minute test. They can move on to the next stage only if they pass the test. If they fail, they must reset for at least one training cycle and redo the test.

The goal for the first 10 minute set at each new kettlebell weight or new exercise is to complete the test with decent and consistent technique from start to finish. At this point, the number of repetitions performed are relatively unimportant compared to the quality of the lifting. However, during the second attempt of each kettlebell weight, the goal should be to get at least one repetition more than the first test.

If the athlete is able to complete all the tests on the first attempt without having to redo any of the cycles, then they have a possible chance of getting a Master of Sport rank with 32kg by the end of their second year. This is a very hard mission to achieve and probably only 1 out of 100 athletes who have attempted this have succeeded. It took me 4 years to become a Master of Sport, but the training method I used wasn't nearly as effective as the one I currently employ.

After 2 years of uninterrupted training and the athlete can handle enough training volume with 32kg, their year-long schedule should be composed of 5-6 training cycles with Long Cycle and Biathlon alternating one after the other. After any 10 minute set with 32kgs, they should always reset to lighter kettlebells.

YEAR # 1					
months	weeks	kettlebell weight	final set	pace	exercise
#1	1	16kg		any	LONG CYCLE
	2				
	3				
	4				
	5		10'		
#2	6	18kg		any	
	7				
	8				
	9		10'		
#3	10	20kg		any	
	11				
	12				
	13		10'		
#4	14	22kg		any	
	15				
	16				
	17				
	18		10'		
#5	19	24kg		any	
	20				
	21				
	22		10'		
#6	23	16kg		any	BIATHLON (Jerk + Snatch)
	24				
	25		10'		
#7	26	18kg		any	
	27				
	28		10'		
	29	20kg		any	
	30				
	31		10'		
#8	32	22kg		any	
	33				
	34				
	35		10'		
#9	36	24kg		any	
	37				
	38				
	39		10'		
#10	40	16kg	10'	any	LONG CYCLE
	41	18kg	7'	any	
	42	20kg	10'	any	
	43	22kg	7'	any	
#11	44	24kg		any	
	45		10'		
	46	26kg		any	
	47				
	48		7'		
#12	49	28kg		any	
	50				
	51				
	52		10'		

YEAR # 2							
		LC kettlebell weight		LC final set			
months	weeks	JERK KB weight	SNATCH KB weight	JERK final set	SNATCH final set	pace	exercise
#1	1	16kg		10'		any	BIATHLON (Jerk + Snatch)
	2	18kg		7'		any	
	3	20kg		10'		any	
	4	22kg		7'		any	
	5	24kg				any	
#2	6			10'			
	7						
	8	26kg				any	
	9			7'			
#3	10						
	11	28kg				any	
	12						
	13			10'			
#4	14	24kg		7'		any	
	15	26kg				any	
	16			7'			
	17	28kg				any	
	18			10'			
#5	19	30kg				any	
	20			7'			
	21						
	22						
#6	23					any	
	24						
	25						
	26						
#7	27						
	28						
	29	from 16kg to 32kg 2 training per weight				any	
	30						
	31			10' set for each weight			
#8	32	20kg	16kg	7'	10'	any	
	33	22kg	18kg	7'	10'	any	
	34	24kg	20kg	10'	10'	any	
	35	26kg	22kg	7'	10'	any	
#9	36	28kg	24kg	10'	10'	any	
	37	30kg	26kg	7'	10'	any	
	38		28kg		10'	any	
	39		30kg		10'	any	
#10	40					any	
	41					any	
	42	22kg		7'		any	
	43	24kg		10'		any	
#11	44	26kg		7'		any	
	45	28kg		10'		any	LONG CYCLE
	46	30kg		7'		any	
	47					any	
	48					any	
#12	49					any	
	50					any	
	51					any	
	52					any	

YEAR # 3 (or any next typical year)							
		LC kettlebell weight		LC final set			
months	weeks	JERK KB weight	SNATCH KB weight	JERK final set	SNATCH final set	pace	exercise
DECEMBER	1	22kg		7'		comp	
	2	24kg		10'		comp	
	3	26kg		7'		comp	
	4	28kg		10'		comp	
	5	30kg		7'		comp	
JANUARY	6					competition	
	7						
	8						
	9						
FEBRUARY	10						
	11						
	12						
	13	16kg	16kg	7'	10'	comp	BIATHLON (Jerk + Snatch)
MARCH	14	18kg	18kg	7'	10'	comp	
	15	20kg	20kg	10'	10'	comp	
	16	22kg	22kg			comp	
	17			7'	10'		
	18		24kg			competition	
APRIL	19				10'		
	20	24kg					
	21						
	22						
MAY	23			10'			
	24	20kg		7'		comp	
	25	22kg		7'		comp	
	26	24kg		10'		comp	
JUNE	27	26kg		7'		comp	
	28	28kg		10'		comp	
	29	30kg		7'		comp	
	30					competition	
	31						
JULY	32						
	33						
	34						
	35						
AUGUST	36						
	37					competition	
	38	from 16kg to 32kg 2 training per weight					
	39						
SEPTEMBER	40			10' set for each weight			
	41	20kg	16kg	7'	10'	comp	
	42	22kg	18kg	7'	10'	comp	
	43	24kg	20kg	10'	10'	comp	
OCTOBER	44	26kg	22kg	7'	10'	comp	
	45	28kg	24kg	10'	10'	comp	
	46	30kg	26kg	7'	10'	comp	
	47					competition	
	48		28kg		10'		
NOVEMBER	49						
	50		30kg		10'		
	51						
	52						

Fig. 26. cont. Denis Vasilev Kettlebell Sport mesocycle

Up to 4 weeks of total rest is allowed during the year, but rather than take it all at once, the better option would be to rest for up to two weeks twice a year with 6 months in between. It's also possible to rest up to 1 week four times a year, preferably after a major competition (10-12 weeks of training + 1 week of rest repeated 4 times). In addition to vacations, I also recommend scheduling a couple of sport massage sessions at the end of each training cycle (4-6 times a year).

During my own career, I never took a full vacation from my workouts. Instead, I chose to do "active rest" by training only the Snatch for a month. It felt refreshing and fairly easy after spending a lot of time working with two kettlebells in Long Cycle and Jerk. I worked my way up from 16kg, spending time on each of the 2kg increments, until I reached 32kg and sometimes I would even stop at 24kg. By training only Snatch, I could still push myself without overworking because this exercise emphasizes cardio and endurance rather than strength.

Kettlebell Sport Workout Structure

A kettlebell sport workout is made up of three main units performed in a particular order. Each unit is further divided into three components and all of them are crucial to getting the most out of your training.

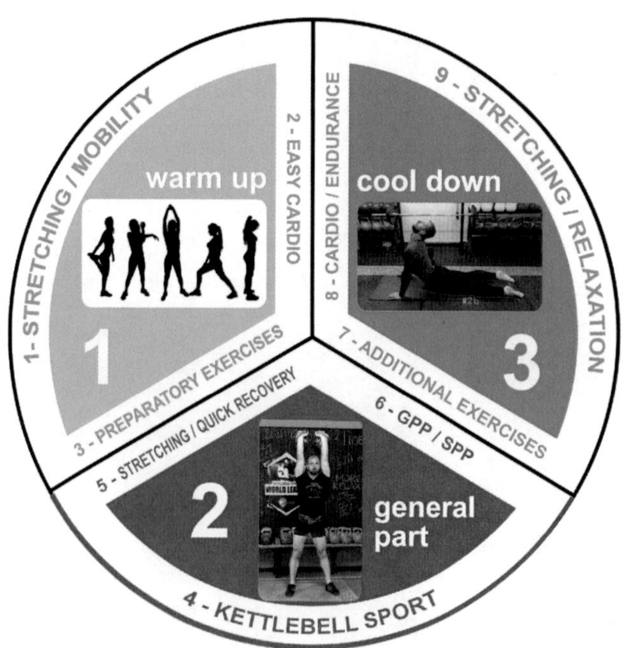

Fig. 27. Kettlebell sport workout structure

If you have limited time, you can cut short the time spent during the General Part but it would be unwise to completely avoid doing the Warm Up and Cool Down. Consistently performing your warm up and cool down will immediately alert you to anything that feels out of place in your body. Both components keep you aware of how everything generally feels regarding the stiffness or suppleness of your joints and muscles, the amount of focus and energy you have, and the status of

> ***"Before starting a workout, you should be able to define in clear terms what you want to achieve for each component."***

your recovery. Skipping these components too often will lead to unnecessary risks that can be easily avoided.

The feeling of your performance during your main kettlebell sport sets will also indicate what other components you might need to work on in order to progress. For example, shoulders that consistently feel tight and stiff during the Jerk are a clear indication that you need to spend more time on stretching and mobility. Early fatigue in the legs during the Cleans might mean you need to start including more leg exercises in your GPP. More commonly, being unable to recover fast enough between working sets is a sure sign that your cardio is not as good as it should be. All these signals will direct you towards where you need to focus on outside of the main sets.

Before starting a workout, you should be able to define in clear terms what you want to achieve for each component. For example, the warm up might be targeted towards improving shoulder flexibility and preparation for overhead lifting. During the main sets you might set the goal of paying attention to a particular detail of the Clean to improve the efficiency of your technique. Subsequently, you might plan to perform a target number of squats with a certain weight to improve your leg strength. And for the cardio component, you might want to complete a certain distance within a specified time.

A kettlebell sport workout has many moving parts and it can be challenging to keep track of all of them. As such, the best thing is to focus only on one target at a time and work progressively towards other challenges that will arise.

Warm Up

It's better to perform a general warm up in a group while under the supervision of a coach or the most advanced athlete in the group. The intensity is moderate and the duration depends on how much time is allotted for the training session, the available space and equipment, the individual training experience of the group members, etc. Distractions should be minimized and the athletes should be arranged so that they can easily hear and see the demonstrations being performed by the person leading the group.

> ***While transitioning between warm up exercises (around 1-3 minutes), you can use the time as active rest by performing mobility, stretching, and breathing exercises that directly benefit the specific joints and muscles used in kettlebell sport lifting such as the elbows, shoulders, upper and lower back, hips, knees, and ankles.***

TYPE OF WORK	TYPICAL EXERCISES	PURPOSE
1. Mobility / Stretching (5-10 minutes) Equipment: Mobility stick, lacrosse ball, Swedish ladder (wall bars), foam roller, exercise ball, resistance rubber bands, Indian clubs, et.	Rotational, swinging and stretching movements as well as massaging and rolling for the neck, wrists, elbows, shoulders, upper back, lower back, pelvis cups, knees and ankles. 5-10 repetitions per exercise	Status check, flexibility improvement for the surrounding joints and muscles.
2. Easy Cardio (5-10 minutes) Equipment: Treadmill, jump rope, rowing machine, indoor / outdoor bike, Elliptical machine, fitness stepper, etc.	Walking, running, jumping, rowing, biking	Raise heart rate to 120-140BPM, breathing activation for the lungs, increase blood circulation and oxygen dispersion, "preheat" the muscles and joints.
3a. General Preparatory (5-10 minutes) Equipment: Pull up bar, back extension machine, pulldown/ cable row machine, lightweight barbell, lightweight kettlebell	Air squats, deadlifts, good mornings, back extensions, pull ups / chin ups, pulldowns, seated cable rows, barbell rows, push-ups 2-3 sets per exercise 10-20 repetitions per set	Muscle activation (lower and upper back, thighs, glutes), relief from soreness, "wake up" problem areas.
3b. Specific Preparatory (10-15 minutes) Equipment: Competition kettlebells from 8kg up to 32kg with 2kg weight increments	One arm Cleans, Swings, Long Cycle, Jerk, Snatch. Double Cleans, Long Cycle, Jerk. 1-2 sets per exercise 5-10 repetitions per set	Develop and improve kettlebell lifting skills, correcting technique mistakes.

A specialized warm up with kettlebells should be done on the platform or lifting area where the athletes will perform their main sets. This has the added benefit of familiarizing the athlete with the surroundings that they will find themselves in while actually lifting. As a general rule, you should warm up with bells up to 8kg lighter than your main sets and increase the weight gradually. For example, if your main sets are with 24kg bells, you should start with 16kg, then 20kg, and work up to 24kg using 2-4kg increments. While transitioning between warm up exercises (around 1-3 minutes),

you can use the time as active rest by performing mobility, stretching, and breathing exercises that directly benefit the specific joints and muscles used in kettlebell sport lifting such as the elbows, shoulders, upper and lower back, hips, knees, and ankles.

Below is an example of my own warm up for the Long Cycle with 32kg.

Warmup mobility exercises for all the parts of the body v(5-7 minutes)
Easy run 1000m or easy rowing 500m
2 rounds 15-20 Back extensions 10 Pull ups
One arm Cleans 16kg / 5+5 repetitions
One arm Long Cycle 16kg / 5+5 repetitions
One arm Cleans 24kg / 5+5 repetitions
One arm Long Cycle 24kg / 5+5 repetitions
One arm Cleans 32kg / 5+5 repetitions
One arm Long Cycle 32kg / 5+5 repetitions
Cleans 32+32kg / 5-7 repetitions
Long Cycle 32+32kg / 30 seconds (10rpm)

General Part

Success in kettlebell sport depends greatly on the coach's knowledge and methodological skill as well as on the student's personal interest and motivation. The demonstration and explanation of proper lifting technique are vital parts of the coaching process and the coach must spend as much time as necessary until the student understands what the coach means to convey. After the demonstration and explanation, the coach must observe that the athlete is able to perform the technique correctly. When practicing in a group of athletes with similar experience and abilities, each can practice individually

TYPE OF WORK	TYPICAL EXERCISES	PURPOSE
4a. Main Kettlebell Sport Exercises (10-30 minutes) Equipment: Competition kettlebells from 8kg up to 32kg with 2kg weight increments.	Sets of Long Cycle, Jerk, and/or Snatch according to your training plan. Average of 10 minutes total of work per discipline throughout the training cycle.	Improvement of kettlebell lifting skills, accumulation of training experience, increase of competition results.
4b. Optional Kettlebell Sport Exercises (10-15 minutes) Equipment: Competition kettlebells from 8kg up to 32kg with 2kg weight increments.	Cleans, swings, static holds, etc. that can be time based (1-10 minutes total) or repetition based (20-100 repetitions total).	Targeted effort at improving technique inefficiencies related to grip endurance, lower back strength, hand insertion, etc.
5. Mobility (as needed) These exercises can be used as active rest in between warm up exercises and kettlebell sport sets. Equipment: Mobility stick, lacrosse ball, Swedish ladder (wall bars), foam roller, exercise ball, resistance rubber bands, Indian clubs, etc.	Rotational, swinging and stretching movements as well as massaging and rolling for the neck, wrists, elbows, shoulders, upper back, lower back, pelvis cups, knees and ankles. 5-10 repetitions per exercise	Provides quick and immediate recovery from muscle tension, aids recovery in between sets, functions as preparation for the upcoming work set, improves joint mobility.
6a. General Physical Preparation (15-30 minutes) Equipment: Power rack, barbell and weights, pull up bar, dip bars, bench, etc.	Other sports such as powerlifting, CrossFit, rowing, track and field (running), gymnastics, etc. Extra attention must be placed on managing the volume based on the chosen sport's training methodology.	Development and improvement of the athlete's general physical qualities (strength, endurance, coordination, etc.).

while the coach observes the group. If there are varying levels of training experience within the group then the coach should approach each person individually.

Safety is the top priority and at no point should the athlete be at risk of injury. If the athlete is unable to correctly and safely perform their sets, then the solution is to immediately switch to lighter weights. If injury or other special conditions prevent the athlete from using kettlebells altogether, the coach should select alternative exercises for the session. Alternatively, the athlete can spend more time working on their mobility or cardio.

The best results in kettlebell sport can be achieved by starting with the lightest weights the athlete can safely handle. Generally speaking this means 12-16kg for males and 4-8kg for females. This allows the athlete to comfortably work on their technique and safely build up their training volume without risking injury from trauma with the heavier bells. As mentioned previously, an entire set of competition kettlebells from 4-32kg with increasing increments of 2kg is indispensable to a serious athlete who wants to reach the highest levels of kettlebell sport.

For every beginning kettlebell athlete, the quality of technique is unequivocally more important than the number of repetitions performed. Fewer but higher quality repetitions are more valuable than many sloppy repetitions. Beginners must not force their results as repetitions simply follow correct and efficient lifting technique. The training load must grow gradually according to the progression of the athlete's skills.

Based on my coaching experience, a new student needs approximately 4-5 weeks with each kettlebell weight to be able to progress safely. For example, an athlete who starts with 16kg and increases by 2kg every month needs at least five months to get to 24kg. In order to move to the next heavier weight, the athlete must complete a 10 minute set with stable lifting technique from start until finish, no matter the repetitions performed. It is only logical that a failed 10 minute set with 22kg does not inspire confidence for a successful 10 minute set with 24kg. In this case the athlete should either drop back to 18kg and build up again or recalibrate their original target of 10 minutes to just 5 minutes with 24kg.

Cool Down

If the Warm Up is your safety check, the Cool Down is your recovery. Without the cool down, your recovery time can double and you might find yourself sore, stiff, and unprepared to perform your next workout. It is extremely important to relieve the stress and tension accumulated during the workout as soon as possible, preferably while your muscles and joints are still warm and your memory is still fresh. While going through your cool down routine, you can spend extra time on specific areas that you feel require additional attention. The duration of your routine can vary depending on the difficulty of your workout. Some days you will need more time to calm down and relax after a challenging set. If possible, I highly recommend spending 5-10 minutes in a sauna or hot shower immediately after the cool down.

TYPE OF WORK	TYPICAL EXERCISES	PURPOSE
7. Additional Exercises (5-30 minutes) Equipment: Depends on the sport / activity of your choice	Exercises not connected with kettlebell sport such as gymnastics, arm wrestling, climbing, bodybuilding, etc.	Satisfaction of personal needs, stress removal, development of additional skills which may indirectly benefit kettlebell sport training.
8. Cardio (10-40 minutes) Equipment: Treadmill, jump rope, rowing machine, indoor / outdoor bike, Elliptical machine, fitness stepper, etc.	Walking, running, jumping, rowing, biking	Development and improvement of aerobic endurance, stabilization of breathing and recovery, relaxation of muscles, mental relaxation. The target heart rate is between 160-180BPM. The pace should be similar to a kettlebell sport set with an easy start, stable middle portion, and strong finish.
9. Stretching (15-30 minutes) Equipment: Yoga mat, foam roller, lacrosse ball, yoga ball, mobility stick, massage gun, etc.	Varying static and dynamic exercises for stretching and flexibility performed while lying down and being seated on the floor. You can view my actual stretching routine online: https://youtu.be/AOHT8pZoQgU	Promotes relaxation, muscle recovery, improvement of joint mobility, and mental stress relief.

PART 2

3

My Time In The Russian National Team

I started analyzing my own performance in kettlebell sport when I was on the Russian National Team from August 2008 until November 2015. I was officially competing in the professional division of the Long Cycle event with two 32kg bells and lifting for 10 minutes. As a member of the national team I was obligated to compete in four main tournaments: the qualifier for the Russian Championships, the Russian Championships itself, the European Championships, and the World Championships. If you are a current champion of Russia and are part of the national team, you are given the option of not participating in the local qualifiers, Russian Cups, European Cups, and World Cups. Thanks to this regulation I was able to focus solely on the four most important competitions mentioned above.

During my career I was able to win six World Championships (IUKL), seven European Championships (IUKL), seven Russian Championships (VFGS), one European Cup (IUKL), three Russian Cups (VFGS), and two qualifiers for the Russian Championships (VFGS)*. I had no mental breakdowns, I never lost my working capacity, and I never broke my training schedule which allowed the training methodology to show its fullest capabilities. Thanks to my training strategy of switching between Long Cycle and Biathlon and by using lighter training weights, I was able to stay mentally and physically fresh throughout my career. I never missed any competition I signed up for, never got sick or injured, and my body weight was always within the range of my weight class. I never lost and I won every single competition. Kettlebell sport was the only priority in my life for eight straight years. I never let my team down.

Awarding ceremony, IUKL World Championship 2013

---

*IUKL (International Union of Kettlebell Lifting), VFGS (Russian Girevoy Sport Federation)

Competitions	Place and dates of the competition	Weight class	Result	Place
		Year 2008		
1. European Championship	Ventspils (Lithuania), August 24th	85kg	87	1st place
2. Cup of Russia	Obninsk, September 16th	80kg	83	1st place
3. World Championship	Smolensk, November 14th	85kg	84	1st place
		Year 2009		
4. European Zone Qualifiers for Russian Championship	Sukko, April 22nd	80kg	82	1st place
5. Championship of Russia	St. Petersburg, June 2nd	80kg	84	1st place
6. European Championship	Pushkin, September 2nd	85kg	81	1st place
		Year 2010		
7 .European Zone Qualifiers for Russian Championship	Novocheboksarsk, April 20th	85kg	81	1st place
8. Championship of Russia	Belgorod, June 2nd	85kg	78	1st place
9. Cup of Russia	Yelets, October 3rd	85kg	79	1st place
10. World Championship	Tampere (Finland), November 13th	85kg	81	1st place
		Year 2011		
11. European Championship	Siauliai (Lithuania), May 22nd	85kg	85	1st place
12. Championship of Russia	Tumen, June 3rd	85kg	80	1st place
13. World Championship	Nanuet (USA), September 18th	85kg	84	1st place
14. Cup of Russia	Yelets, October 12th	85kg	74	1st place
		Year 2012		
15. European Championship	Belgorod, May 19th	85kg	82	1st place
16. Championship of Russia	Orenburg, June 10th	85kg	83	1st place
		Year 2013		
17. European Championship	Wexford (Ireland), May 26th	85kg	83	1st place
18. Championship of Russia	Omsk, June 1st	85kg	83	1st place
19. World Championship	Tumen, November 23rd	85kg	90	1st place
		Year 2014		
20. European Championship	Pushkin, May 14th	85kg	90	1st place
21. Championship of Russia	Kirov, June 3rd	85kg	89	1st place
22 .World Championship	Hamburg (Germany), Nov 23rd	85kg	91	1st place
		Year 2015		
23. Cup of Europe	Peterhof, May 24th	85kg	81	1st place
24. Championship of Russia	Lomonosov, May 29th	85kg	84	1st place
25. European Championship	Varna (Bulgaria), July 13th	85kg	87	1st place
26. World Championship	Dublin (Ireland), Nov 28th	85kg	90	1st place

Fig. 28. List of professional victories

I was also very lucky during this time because international interest in kettlebell sport was starting to grow and, being one of the highest-level lifters at the time, I was invited to teach kettlebell sport in different countries. I visited and taught in twenty countries including Australia, Brazil, Bulgaria, Canada, Chile, China, Croatia, Denmark, England, Germany, Indonesia, Ireland, Japan, Mexico, Poland, Puerto Rico, Russia, Sweden, Switzerland, and the USA. This amazing experience kept me motivated and happy so it was easy for me to sustain my mental and emotional enthusiasm. It was also relatively easy to stay in shape while I was travelling since all the locations I taught at had kettlebells that I could train with. My interest in coaching and lifting was definitely stimulated during this period.

Looking back on all my competition results, my lowest was 74 repetitions and the highest was 91 repetitions (with an average of 83.7 repetitions over 26 competitions in the 85kg weight class). According to the VFGS Sport Ranking Tables back in 2015, the requirement for the highest rank of Master of Sport International Class in my weight class was 78 repetitions. My average result exceeded this number by 5.7 repetitions (7.3%) and my best result exceeded it by 13 repetitions (15.3%).

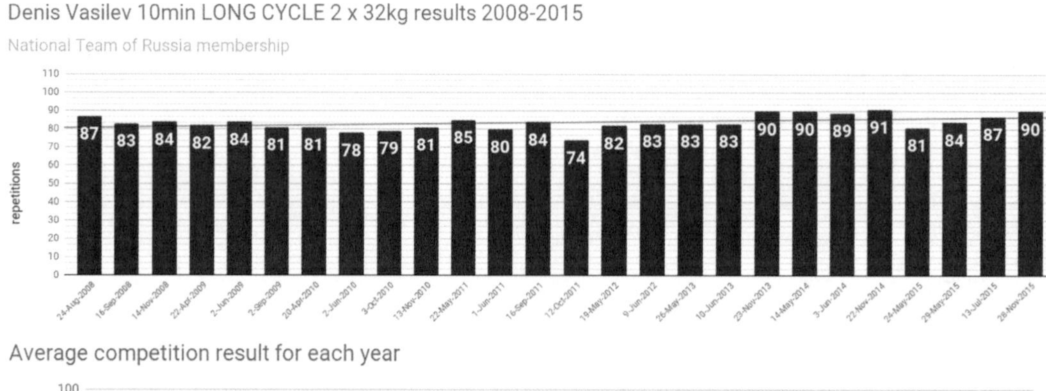

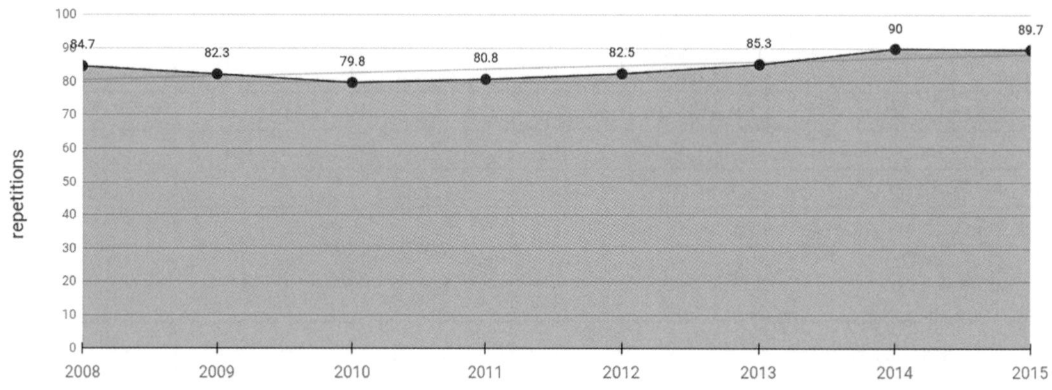

Fig.29. Table of professional 10min Long Cycle 2x32kg and yearly average results (2008-2015)

My success can be attributed to my consistent hard work of trying to incrementally improve my lifting technique, flexibility, cardio, strength endurance, and by trying out different mental strategies. However, I can now unquestionably point to the effectiveness of my training methods which included competent strategic planning, setting realistic training priorities, correct tactical planning, while taking into account all the other objective and subjective factors outside of kettlebell sport. In other words, I was able to create and follow my own personalized training plan based on the principles of my methodology.

Years of accumulated experience also had a huge influence on my results. Kettlebell sport is a cyclical sport and I consider one of the best ways to determine an athlete's training experience is to quantify how many total repetitions he or she has performed in their lifetime. For example, an athlete who has performed 150,000 total repetitions is vastly more experienced and skilled than another athlete who only has 100,000 repetitions under their belt. It also goes without saying that the quality of those repetitions is critical. Technically correct reps reinforce proper muscle memory and actually allow the athlete to handle more volume because they have become more efficient. Poorly executed repetitions establish incorrect and unsafe lifting habits that will endanger the athlete and significantly slow down their progress. The more entrenched these bad habits are, the more difficult it will be to undo the harm done to the athlete. My advice is to work on perfect technique now, not later. Annually, my number of repetitions from Long Cycle, Jerk, and Snatch combined is anywhere between 16,000-17,000, which yields around 900 tons of total work done. However, my first priority will always be perfection of technique and I'm still looking for ways to constantly improve.

From the methodological point of view, my own programming has become more subtle over the years. Since I began lifting in 2001, I've been keeping meticulous records of my training and adding to my "knowledge bank" every year. By 2015, I had accumulated a total of 240,000 repetitions and about 13,500 tons of total volume. Incidentally, that was the year I was able to achieve my dream of doing 101 repetitions in Long Cycle with 32kg. To date, this has been my best performance during my entire career. This is consistent with what I have observed with other elite kettlebell lifters who have put up their best performances after accumulating a similar amount of reps and total volume.

Fig.30. 101 reps 10min Long Cycle 2x32kg in 10min
(Photo credit to @fedyck fotos by Rik Fedyck)

4
My Kettlebell Sport Journey

I can trace the first stage of my career beginning all the way back to my hometown of Kaliningrad, Russia. From 1999 until 2005, I worked my way from being a beginner to a professional. At the time I was only competing in Biathlon with 24kg and was focused on attaining my Candidate Master of Sport rank. All the city competitions I joined back then did not include Long Cycle as a discipline and the first time I was able to compete in Long Cycle was during a national competition in 2001. By August 2005, I got my Master of Sport rank in both Long Cycle (70 repetitions) and Biathlon (184 points, Jerk 114 repetitions, Snatch 142 repetitions).

The methodology I was following back then was completely different. We didn't have access to 2kg increment bells and most of the workouts were done with 32kg. We only used 24kg to train in the off-season for local competitions. It was nearly impossible to work on improving lifting technique and accumulating training volume was very difficult. However, under these conditions I was able to develop great strength and a very tough mental attitude. Kettlebell sport lifting was done alongside weightlifting and powerlifting type training sessions with an emphasis on low repetitions and heavy weight.

I took a break from kettlebell sport from August 2005 until September 2007. During this time I didn't touch kettlebells at all. I was happy to have achieved my goal of becoming a Master of Sport and did not think any more about continuing. As I realized years later, my training routine was quite exhausting and not well-organized which made me not enjoy the process. I became interested in arm wrestling and immediately began a supervised program as soon as I was able to find an internationally ranked coach. However, I quickly realized that the training for professional arm wrestling was not to my liking and I stopped.

Fig. 31. Bodybuilding and powerlifting

Around October 2005, I started digging into Arnold Schwarzenegger's bodybuilding encyclopedia. I was consistently working out hard and gained significant size and strength. My body weight went from 87kg to 95kg over the course of two years of training. By early 2007 my maxes in the gym were: bench press 150kg, back squat 200kg, deadlift 205kg.

The first year of my weight lifting training was exciting and easy in terms of endurance because of my experience in kettlebell sport. Before long, I began to miss kettlebell sport and I thought about going back to training to earn my Master of Sport International Class rank. All the circumstances seemed right to me because I felt stronger physically and I was mentally fresh to work towards a new achievement. I also happened to be living in the right place because Saint Petersburg was home to one of the greatest kettlebell sport teams in Russia, with multiple-time Russian and World champions among their members.

This was the backdrop for the second stage of my journey in kettlebell sport. I was living in Saint Petersburg from 2005 until 2017 and this was the peak of my career as a member of the Russian National Team. Without the initial introduction of my friend and teammate Eduard Ahramenko (Kaliningrad), I would not have had the good fortune to become accepted into the circle of legendary sportsmen and champions including Arkady Semyonov (St. Petersburg), Sergey Rachinsky (St. Petersburg), Valery Litvinko (St. Petersburg), Sergey Rudnev (Blagoveschensk), Sergey Merkulin (Belgorod), Igor Novikov (Yelets), and many others. These great men were extremely kind and supportive and they were always open in sharing their coaching and lifting experiences. At the time, their training methods were already considered to be the most advanced and effective for specialized physical preparation in kettlebell

Fig. 32. Upper left (me, Rachinsky, Ahramenko), upper right (me, Rachinsky), lower left (me), lower right (me, Merkulin, Rudnev, Rachinsky)

sport. It was impossible not to become a champion in such an environment of constant inspiration and motivation. I initially thought I would need at least a year to recover my form for Master of Sport in Long Cycle and then another year after that to work towards Master of Sport International Class. As it happened, I was able to become the European champion and world record holder in 2008 with the result of 90 repetitions (3 no counts), far exceeding the requirement for MSIC rank.

I am now in the third stage of my career working in Oakland, California as a full-time kettlebell sport coach. I am officially retired from the national team but I still consider myself as a professional athlete and I have been able to maintain the results necessary for Master of Sport International Class. Since I now have the option to choose which competitions and events I want to participate in, I was able to work on my Biathlon results and increase my numbers to the level of MSIC. After having achieved this rank for both disciplines, I can honestly tell myself that I am a complete expert in kettlebell sport and this gives me even more confidence in my training methodology. My own results are proof that it works for all three kettlebell sport exercises.

Fig 33. Upper left (John Buckley, Jason Dobly, me, Aaron Guyett), lower left (Jason Dobly, me, John Buckley), right (me)

Long Cycle Results

I did my very first Long Cycle competition with 32kg on February 23 2001 and ended up with a laughable 17 repetitions. Since then, I've done a total of sixty six 10 minute sets with an average result of 80.4 repetitions. Fifty of those were performed with a result higher than the requirement for Master of Sport International Class.

10min Long Cycle 2 x 32kg Competitions and GYM tests from 2001 till 2021
by Denis Vasilev, MSIC, 85kg weight class

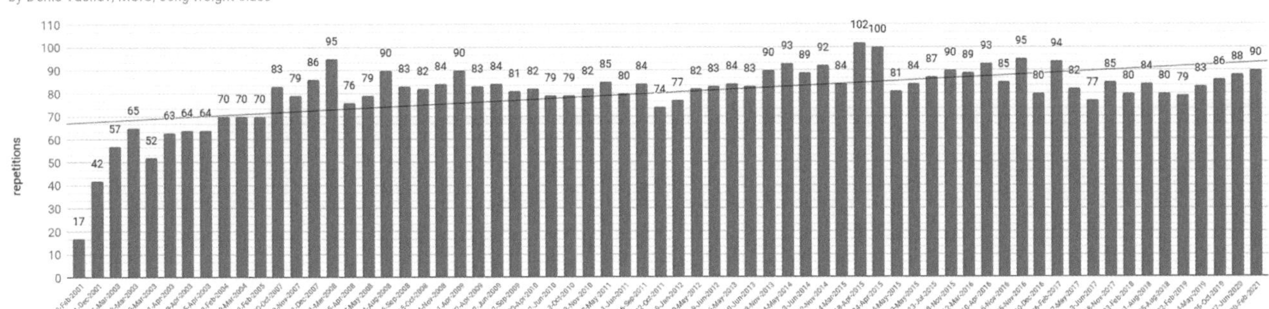

Fig. 34. Chart of 10min Long Cycle 2x32kg and yearly average results (2001-2021) part 1

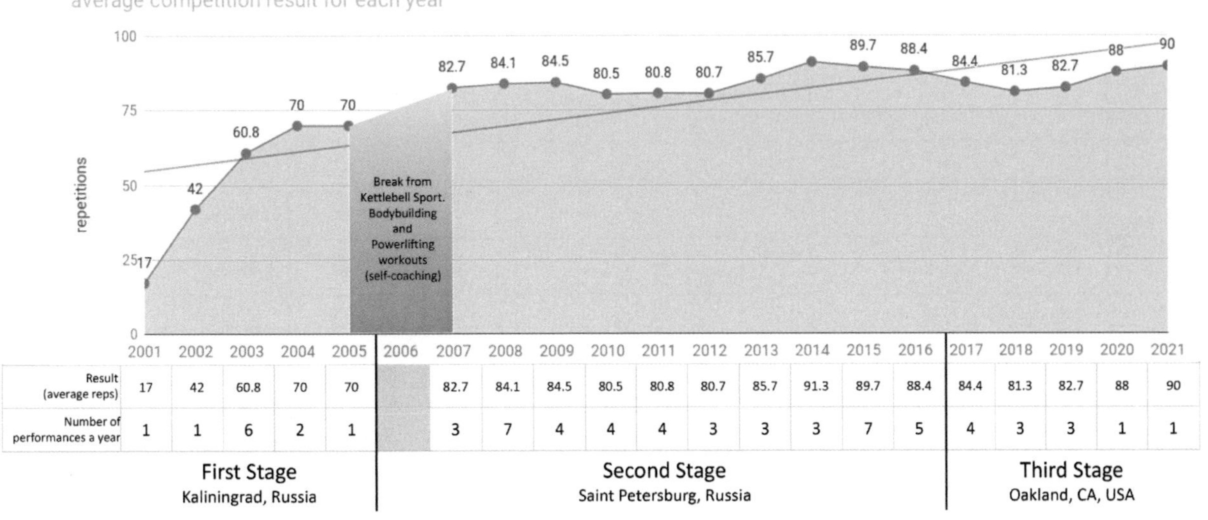

	2001	2002	2003	2004	2005	2006	2007	2008	2009	2010	2011	2012	2013	2014	2015	2016	2017	2018	2019	2020	2021
Result (average reps)	17	42	60.8	70	70		82.7	84.1	84.5	80.5	80.8	80.7	85.7	91.3	89.7	88.4	84.4	81.3	82.7	88	90
Number of performances a year	1	1	6	2	1		3	7	4	4	4	3	3	3	7	5	4	3	3	1	1

Fig. 34. Chart of 10min Long Cycle 2x32kg and yearly average results (2001-2021) part 2

NOTES	REPS	DATE	EVENT	PLACE	RANK		YEAR
4min	17	23-Feb-2001	Saint Petersburg competition, Russia	2nd place	**none**	1	**2001**
7min	42	1-Dec-2001	Saint Petersburg competition, Russia	1st place	**Rank I**	1	**2002**
7min 30sec	57	1-Mar-2003	Kaliningrad Oblast Championship, Kaliningrad, Russia	1st place	**CMS**	1	**2003 60.8 reps average**
	65	18-Mar-2003	GYM test		**MS**	2	
9min 30sec	52	29-Mar-2003	Juniors Championship of Russia, Babaevo, Russia	3rd place	**CMS**	3	
	63	11-Apr-2003	GYM test		**MS**	4	
	64	18-Apr-2003	GYM test		**MS**	5	
	64	25-Apr-2003	GYM test		**MS**	6	
9min	70	28-Feb-2004	Kaliningrad Oblast Championship, Kaliningrad, Russia	1st place	**MS**	1	**2004 70 reps average**
	70	28-Mar-2004	Championship of Russia, Smolensk, Russia	7th place	**MS**	2	
8min 20sec	70	12-Feb-2005	Kaliningrad Oblast Championship, Kaliningrad, Russia	1st place	**MS**	1	**2005**
Horizontal Bench press 1rep PR - 150kg							**Aug 2005 to Sept 2007**
Barbell Back Squats 1rep PR - 200kg							
Barbell Dead Lift 1rep PR - 200kg							
	83	20-Oct-2007	Leningrad Oblast Championship, Gatchina, Russia	1st place	**MSIC**	1	**2007 82.7 reps average**
	79	23-Nov-2007	Saint Petersburg Championship, Russia	1st place	**MS**	2	
	86	1-Dec-2007	GYM test		**MSIC**	3	
	95	21-Mar-2008	GYM test		**MSIC**	1	**2008 84.1 reps average**
5 no counts	76	15-Apr-2008	European Zone Qualifiers for Russian Championship, Voronezsh, Russia	4th place	**MS**	2	
	79	27-May-2008	Championship of Russia, Surgut, Russia	2nd place	**MS**	3	
3 no counts	90	24-Aug-2008	European Championship (IUKL), Ventspils, Latvia	1st place	**MSIC**	4	
	83	16-Sep-2008	Cup of Russia, Obninsk, Russia	1st place	**MSIC**	5	
1 no count	82	15-Oct-2008	Moscow competition, Russia	1st place	**MSIC**	6	
	84	14-Nov-2008	World Championship (IUKL), Smolensk, Russia	1st place	**MSIC**	7	
	90	1-Apr-2009	GYM test		**MSIC**	1	**2009 84.5 reps average**
1 no count	83	22-Apr-2009	European Zone Qualifiers for Russian Championship, Sukko, Russia	1st place	**MSIC**	2	
	84	2-Jun-2009	Championship of Russia, Saint Petersburg, Russia	1st place	**MSIC**	3	
	81	2-Sep-2009	European Championship (IUKL), Saint Petersburg, Russia	1st place	**MSIC**	4	

1 no count	82	20-Apr-2010	European Zone Qualifiers for Russian Championship, Novocheboksarsk, Russia	1st place	**MSIC**	1	**2010 80.5 reps average**
1 no count	79	2-Jun-2010	Championship of Russia, Belgorod, Russia	1st place	**MSIC**	2	
	79	3-Oct-2010	Cup of Russia, Elec, Russia	1st place	**MSIC**	3	
1 no count	82	13-Nov-2010	World Championship (IUKL), Tampere, Finland	1st place	**MSIC**	4	
	85	22-May-2011	European Championship (IUKL), Siauliai, Lithuania	1st place	**MSIC**	1	**2011 80.8 reps average**
	80	1-Jun-2011	Championship of Russia, Tumen, Russia	1st place	**MSIC**	2	
	84	16-Sep-2011	World Championship (IUKL), Nanuet, NY, USA	1st place	**MSIC**	3	
	74	12-Oct-2011	Cup of Russia, Elec, Russia	1st place	**MS**	4	
	77	19-Jan-2012	GYM test		**MSIC**		**2012 80.7 reps average**
	82	19-May-2012	European Championship (IUKL), Belgorod, Russia	1st place	**MSIC**		
	83	9-Jun-2012	Championship of Russia, Orenburg, Russia	1st place	**MSIC**		
1 no count	84	26-May-2013	European Championship (IUKL), Wexford, Ireland	1st place	**MSIC**	1	**2013 85.7 reps average**
	83	10-Jun-2013	Championship of Russia, Omsk, Russia	1st place	**MSIC**	2	
	90	23-Nov-2013	World Championship (IUKL), Tumen, Russia	1st place	**MSIC**	3	
3 no counts	93	14-May-2014	European Championship (IUKL), Saint Petersburg, Russia	1st place	**MSIC**	1	**2014 91.3 reps average**
	89	3-Jun-2014	Championship of Russia, Kirov, Russia	1st place	**MSIC**	2	
1 no count	92	22-Nov-2014	World Championship (IUKL), Hamburg, Germany	1st place	**MSIC**	3	
	84	14-Mar-2015	Puerto Rico Championship, San Juan	1st place	**MSIC**	1	**2015 89.7 reps average**
1 no count	**102**	18-Apr-2015	Vancouver Open Championship, Canada	1st place	**MSIC**	2	
	100	24-Apr-2015	White Nights Championship, Saint Petersburg, Russia	1st place	**MSIC**	3	
	81	24-May-2015	Cup of Europe (IUKL), Peterhof, Russia	1st place	**MSIC**	4	
	84	29-May-2015	Championship of Russia, Lomonosov, Russia	1st place	**MSIC**	5	
	87	13-Jul-2015	European Championship (IUKL), Varna, Bulgaria	1st place	**MSIC**	6	
	90	28-Nov-2015	World Championship (IUKL), Dublin, Ireland	1st place	**MSIC**	7	
	89	12-Mar-2016	Puerto Rico Championship, San Juan	1st place	**MSIC**	1	**2016 88.4 reps average**
	93	10-Apr-2016	Shanghai Championship, China	1st place	**MSIC**	2	
	85	5-Nov-2016	World Championship (IKFF), Novi, MI, USA	1st place	**MSIC**	3	
	95	25-Nov-2016	Japan Championship, Tokyo	1st place	**MSIC**	4	
	80	10-Dec-2016	Brazil Championship, Sao Paulo	1st place	**MSIC**	5	

	94	26-Feb-2017	World Championship (WAKSC), Costa Mesa, CA, USA	1st place	**MSIC**	1	**2017 84.4 reps average**
	82	27-May-2017	White Nights Championship, Saint-Petersburg, Russia	1st place	**MSIC**	2	
	77	3-Jun-2017	Amber Kettlebells Competition, Kaliningrad, Russia	1st place	**MS**	3	
	85	18-Nov-2017	World Championship (IKFF), Novi, MI, USA	1st place	**MSIC**	4	
	80	23-Feb-2018	World Championship (IKO), Costa Mesa, CA, USA	1st place	**MSIC**	1	**2018 81.3 reps average**
	84	11-Aug-2018	Northern California Open Competition, Berkeley, CA, USA	1st place	**MSIC**	2	
	80	25-Aug-2018	European Championship (IKO), Olsztyn, Poland	1st place	**MSIC**	3	
	79	22-Feb-2019	World Championship (IKO), Costa Mesa, CA, USA	1st place	**MSIC**	1	**2019 82.7 reps average**
	83	4-May-2019	Great Plaints Competition, Wichita, KS, USA	1st place	**MSIC**	2	
	86	26-Oct-2019	World Championship (IKFF), Novi, MI, USA	1st place	**MSIC**	3	
	88	27-Jun-2020	USA Nationals (IKO), ONLINE	1st place	**MSIC**	1	**2020**
	90	20-Feb-2021	World Championship (IKO), ONLINE	1st place	**MSIC**	2	**2021**

Fig. 36. Table of 10min Long Cycle 2x32kg sets (2001-2021)

I haven't counted all the other 10min sets I've done with lighter weights, but below is a chart showing my top two best results for every kettlebell weight I've ever used. I consider Long Cycle to be my favorite discipline and it's not a coincidence that it's also my most successful and accomplished lift.

Denis Vasilev Personal Records												
10min Long Cycle (two kettlebells), reps												
	16kg	**18kg**	**20kg**	**22kg**	**24kg**	**26kg**	**28kg**	**30kg**	**32kg**	**33kg**	**34kg**	**40kg**
second best	160	165	154	155	147	106	116	101	100	61 (6')	61 (6')	50 (9')
actual	**168**	**221 (18')**	**160**	**170 (14')**	**150**	**124**	**120**	**104**	**102**	**62 (6')**	**61 (6')**	**57**
	17 rpm	16 rpm	16 rpm	15 rpm	15 rpm	12 rpm	12 rpm	10 rpm	10 rpm	10 rpm	10 rpm	6 rpm

Fig. 37. Current long cycle records (2021)

Indeed, th majority of my recognizable titles and achievements were in Long Cycle. However, I did not always have a comfortable time with this exercise. During the early stages of my career I was dealing with technique issues related to the Rack Position and Top Fixation. Both static positions felt extremely uncomfortable and I often received several no-counts during competition. My competition results also suffered because I was lifting slower than my training pace. For instance, I was already hitting pace 10 in training since 2007, but it was not until 2013 that I was able to perform 90 repetitions at the World Championships in Tyumen, Russia. This provided me with huge motivation to work even harder to demonstrate beautiful repetitions that would leave no doubt in the judge's mind about the quality of my lifting.

The competitions organized by the IUKL are known for having the strictest lifting technique standards. With more lenient judging, I could have gone faster by at least 1 repetition per minute. Eventually, I was able to maintain pace 10 in competition when I competed in Vancouver, Canada on April 18 2015. I did 102 repetitions. What amazes me even more is that less than a week later, on April 24, I was able to repeat my performance in Saint Petersburg, Russia where I did 100 repetitions after a long transatlantic flight from Canada to Russia. My dream of hitting 100 repetitions in competition finally became a reality!

day				
28	Jerk 32kg	10'	9rpm	14,13,13, ... total 130reps
	Snatch 32kg	10' Right first	20rpm	R110+L80. Total 190reps
	California Open Championship/ WAKSC World Championship			BIATHLON score 225pts

MESOCYCLE	MICROCYCLES	Training Method	day	**LONG CYCLE 2 x 32kg TRAINING CYCLE for 100 reps**			
				Jerk			
				KB Weight	kind of work	given pace	completed
				March 2015			
DRAW-IN mesocycle			1				
	Recovery	Flat	2	**LC 20kg**	**6'**	**12rpm**	12,13,14,14,16,17. total 86rp
			3				
		Interval	4	LC 22kg, 24kg	4', 1' (4' rest)	12rpm	**12,12,14,16. total 54rp, 17rp**
			5				
		Interval - Variable	6	LC 22kg, 24kg, Jerk 32kg	4', 3' (4' rest) 20rp(1'10"")	12rpm	11,12,12,13/ 11, 12, 16
			7				
			8	OA Cleans 32kg	Left first	50L+50R	L50+R50 Total 100reps
	Refining	Interval - Variable	9	LC 24kg, 26kg, Jerk 32kg	5', 2' (5' rest) 20rp	12rpm	12rpm
			10				
		Interval	11	LC 26kg, 28kg, 30kg, 32kg	2' x 4sets (2'rest)	10rpm	**10rpm**
			12	Flight to Puerto Rico			
		Competing	13	**32kg**	**4'**	**6-7rpm**	**6,7,8,9. total 30reps**
		Competing	**14**	**LC 32kg**	**10'**	**6-7rpm**	**7,7,7,7,7,8,8,9,10,14. total 84rp**
				Snatch 24kg	**10'**	**20-22rpm**	**215rp**
				Puerto Rico Kettlebell Sport Championship, San Juan			

Mesocycle	Phase	Type	Day	Exercise	Time	Pace	Result
DRAW-IN mesocycle			15	Snatch 24kg		100rp	4'45"
			16				
			17				
			18	Flight to Russia			
	Draw-in	Interval - Variable	19	LC 28kg, 30kg OA Cleans, 32kg	3', 2' (3'rest) 6' Left first	10rpm 20rpm	10rpm L56+R56 Total 112rp in 6'
			20				
		Time Ladder DOWN - Variable	21	LC 30kg, 32kg, 33kg **OA Cleans, 32kg**	3', 2', 1' (3', 2'rest) **8' Left first**	10rpm **20rpm**	10,10,11 / 10,11 / 14 **L72+R78** **Total 150reps**
			22				
	Laborious # 1	Flat	23	**LC 29kg** **OA Cleans, 32kg**	**6'** **8' Right first**	**10rpm** **20rpm**	**10,10,10,10,11,15. total 66rp** **R81+L81** **total 162reps**
			24				
BASELINE mesocycle		Repetative - Variable	25	LC 30kg, 32kg **OA Cleans, 32kg**	4', 3' (4'-5' rest) **Right first**	10rpm **100R + 100L**	10,10,10,12 / 10,10,12 **R100+L100** **Total 200reps**
			26				
		Interval	27	LC 32kg	1' x 7sets (1' rest)	14rpm	14,14,14,14,15,15,15+1
			28				
			29				
	Laborious # 2	Repetative	30	LC 33kg **OA Cleans, 32kg**	4', 3' (4'-5'rest) **10' Left first**	10rpm **20rpm**	10,10,10,10/ 10,10,12 **L101+R103** **total 204reps**
			31				
		April 2015					
		Flat	1	LC 33kg **OA Cleans, 32kg**	5' **Right first**	10rpm **120R, 120L**	10,10,10,10,12. total 52reps **R6'24", L6'44**
			2				
		Interval	3	LC 33kg **OA Cleans, 32kg**	2' x 4sets (2' rest) **12' Left first**	12rpm **20rpm**	12,12/ 12,12/ 12,12 /12,14 **L120+R120 total 240**
			4				
			5				

BASE mesocycle cont.	Laborious # 3	Flat	6	**LC 28kg** **OA Cleans 32kg**	**8′ video** **Left first**	**11rpm** **140L, 140R**	**12, 12, 12, 12, 12, 12, 12, 14+2. total 100rp** **L8’41”, R7’21”**
			7				
		Interval	8	LC 33kg	1′ x 10sets (1′rest)	12rpm	13 / 13 / 13 / 13 / 13 / 13 / 13 / 13 / 13 / 15
			9				
			10				
		Repetative - Variable	11	LC 34kg, 35kg OA Cleans, 32kg	4′, 3′ (7′ rest) 7’R, 7’L (7’ rest)	10rpm 20rpm	10,10,10,11 / 10,10,12 R141rp, L141rp
			12				
PRE-COMPETITION mesocycle	Refining	Flat	14	**LC 33kg** **OA Cleans 32kg**	**6′** **Right first**	**10rpm** **160R, 160L**	**10, 10, 10, 10, 10, 12. total 62rp** **R8’30, L9’30”**
			14				
		Interval	16	LC 33kg OA Cleans, 32kg	3′, 2′ (3′ rest) 8’L, 8’R (7’ rest)	10rpm 20rpm	10,10,10 / 11,12 L164rp, R165rp
			17	Flight to Canada			
	Competing		**18**	LC 32kg	10′	10rpm	**10, 10, 10, 10, 10, 10, 10, 10, 10, 12.** **Total 102reps**
	Refining			OKCI Vancouver Open Kettlebell Sport Competition 2015			
			19	OA Cleans 32kg	10’R, 10’L 7’rest)	20rpm	R 201rp, L 201rp
			20	Flight to Russia			
			21				
		Flat	22	LC 33kg	4’	10rpm	10rpm
			23				
	Competing		**24**	**LC 32kg**	**10′**	**10rpm**	**10, 10, 10, 10, 10, 10, 10, 9, 10, 11.** **Total 100reps**
			25	WAKSC White Nights of Saint-Petersburg Championships 2015			

Fig. 38. 100rp Long Cycle 2x32kg program

My preparation to get 100 repetitions in 10 minutes began right after I achieved my then best resultsn Biathlon during the Cali Open with 130 repetitions in Jerk, 190 repetitions in Snatch, and a Biathlon total of 225 points. I was feeling strong, injury-free, and in very high spirits. I was in such good shape that I was able to get a significantly higher result than what my coach programmed for me when I did an exhibition competition in Puerto Rico only 2 weeks after my Biathlon competition. Sergey had written for me to go at a comfortable pace 6-7 but it was so easy that I couldn't resist picking up the pace after the first 5 minutes of the set and I ended up with 84 repetitions! This was another example where, as I previously mentioned, a Biathlon specialist in great shape would be able to casually compete in Long Cycle with minimal preparation and expect to get 80-90% of his best Long Cycle result.

Another surprising detail about this particular training cycle was that the original plan was to make a strike for 100 repetitions at the WAKSC White Nights Championship in Saint Petersburg, Russia 8 weeks after my Biathlon performance. We also had already taken into consideration that I would be flying to Vancouver, Canada 1 week before competition to do a 5 minute exhibition set. Those were busy and hectic times as I had just graduated from university and the process of procuring a visa did not go as easily as I hoped. In fact, I thought I would miss my flight entirely because I received my visa only 2 hours prior to departure! The best thing I could remember about the whole situation was that I did not have any time to worry about my performance. I was calm and the only thought in my mind was to follow my coach's programming. I was just happy that I was able to make it to Canada for the competition!

As it happened, I found myself in an extraordinarily good mood while I was warming up for my planned 5 minute set. I told myself that I would just maintain pace 10 until the fifth minute with no acceleration, and that I would try to make myself comfortable on pace 10 for as long as I could after that. By the time I hit the fifth minute, everything felt great. I wasn't behind on my count and I wasn't struggling or fighting to maintain pace 10. It just felt so natural. When I got to the eighth minute I finally knew that I would be able to achieve my goal on that day. The ninth minute felt as easy as all the previous ones and on the tenth I was even able to hit 12 repetitions with zero fatigue in the grip. I was able to do 102 repetitions but the counter failed on the final repetition so my official result was 101 repetitions*. It was a great set and I would even argue that it was the most comfortable set I had ever done!

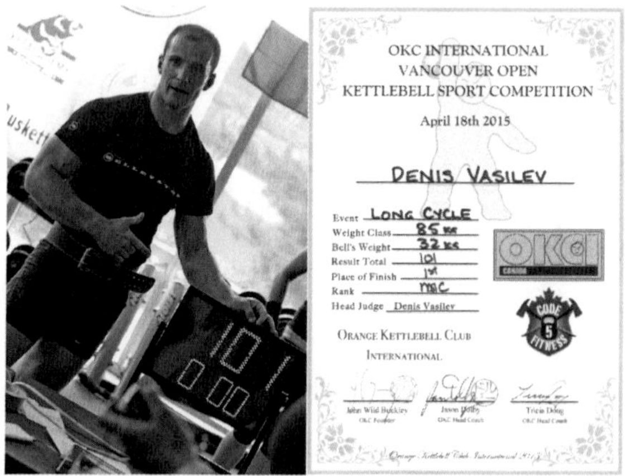

Fig. 39. 101rp Long Cycle 2x32kg diploma

---

* OKC International Vancouver Open KB Sport Competition (April 18 2015 - Vancouver, Canada): https://youtu.be/sI6oLOUvjgU

I had just achieved my lifelong goal of hitting 100 repetitions in 10 minutes a full week before the scheduled competition in Saint Petersburg. I could have stopped there, but the fact that it felt so easy pushed me to try and repeat my performance a week later when I was back in Russia. I only did one workout prior to the competition and immediately afterwards I felt the physical and mental fatigue start to creep in. Still, it wasn't too bad and I was still very much excited to get another 100 repetitions right in front of my coach.

During the competition, right when I cleaned the bells off the platform, I knew I was in trouble. The bells felt unusually heavy and I realized how much of a bad idea it was to try for another 100 repetitions in such a short time frame. Still, it was too late for me to back out because my coach, Sergey Rachinsky, and Sergey Kirillov, the Head Coach of the Russian National Team, were sitting in the audience along with all of my teammates and friends. This gave me a strong motivation to deliver what I had promised.

The first two minutes went well enough, but every minute after that turned into a nightmare. Each minute got tighter as it became more difficult to squeeze in 10 repetitions within each minute and each repetition felt like it would be my last. In the ninth minute I felt that maintaining my current pace of 10 reps per minute would not allow me to handle the final minute well so I made the decision to drop to pace 9. This decision to slow down gave me just enough power to battle through my rapidly fatiguing grip and get 11 repetitions in the final minute, allowing me to get exactly 100 repetitions*. Doing these two performances back to back was the most epic thing I've done during my competitive career and I'm very proud to have achieved it!

Fig. 40. 100rp Long Cycle 2x32kg

---

* WAKSC White Nights Championships (April 24 2015 - Saint Petersburg, Russia)): https://youtu.be/WAX4TUUoCpw

Jerk Result

I did my very first 10 minute Jerk set with 32kg on April 15 2003 with the result of 82 repetitions. Since then, I've done a total of thirty 10 minute sets with an average result of 114.3 repetitions. Five of those were performed with a result higher than 140 repetitions, with the highest result of 145 repetitions performed on August 17 2019.

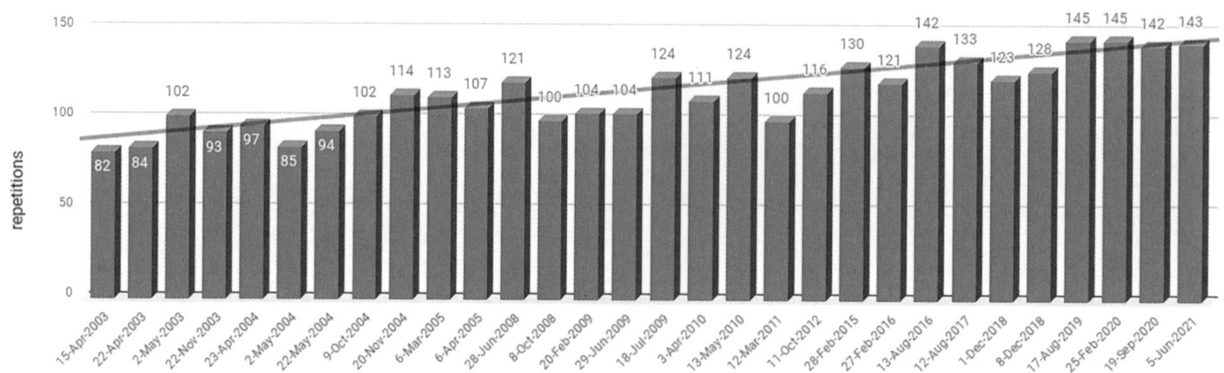

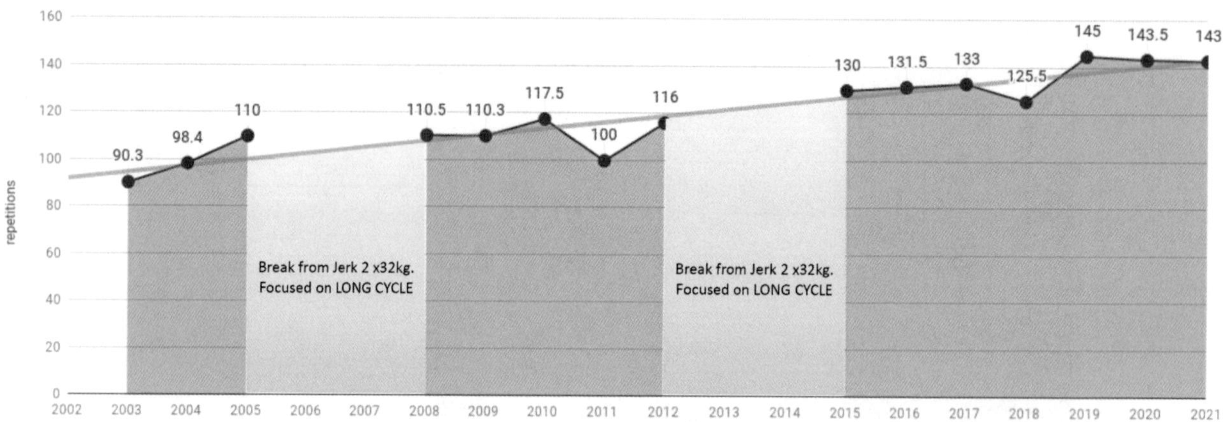

Fig. 41. Chart of 10min Jerk 2x32kg (2001-2021)

I haven't counted all the other 10 minute Jerk sets I've done with lighter weights, but below is a chart showing my top two best results for every kettlebell weight I've ever used.

Denis Vasilev Personal Records									
10min Jerk (two kettlebells), reps									
	16kg	**18kg**	**20kg**	**22kg**	**24kg**	**26kg**	**28kg**	**30kg**	**32kg**
second best	235		230		208		163	139	143
actual	**250**	**230**	**232**	**225**	**210**	**181**	**183**	**164**	**145**
	25 rpm	23 rpm	23 rpm	22-23 rpm	21 rpm	18 rpm	18 rpm	16 rpm	15 rpm

Fig. 42. Current jerk records (2021)

Early in my career from 1999 until 2001, I only competed in Biathlon with 24kg because I was still an amateur lifter and all my competitions were held in the city of Kaliningrad, Russia. Back then there were no Long Cycle competitions. Only after 2001 was the yearly training and competition calendar divided into two main seasons leading up to the Russian Championships. The Long Cycle Championships were held in spring and the Biathlon Championships were in Autumn. I spent half of the year preparing for Long Cycle and the other half preparing for Biathlon. My jerk technique was much better than my snatch back then and I was able to get my Master of Sport rank on November 22 2003 on the strength of my jerk.

From 2008 to 2012 I was focused on achieving my MSIC rank in Long Cycle. As a result, my jerk technique suffered to the point that I always felt discomfort in my lower back whenever I attempted this exercise with 32kg. I felt fine when I was using 24kg but it started to become uncomfortable when I started using heavier weights. As a result, I did not do any jerk training with 32kg from 2013 to 2014 but I continued working on my technique by using lighter training weights. At the end of 2014, I was once again ready to tackle the jerk with 32kg. My investment of going back to lighter weights paid off when I was able to perform 130 repetitions without touching those weights for 2 years. This was the beginning of my success in Jerk and in 2016 I was able to do 140 repetitions without any discomfort in my lower back. I'm now confident that the Jerk is a very safe exercise, even with 32kgs, so long as the correct lifting technique is implemented.

REPS	DATE	EVENT	PLACE	RANK	YEAR
82	15-Apr-2003	GYM test		1	**2003 90.3 reps average**
84	22-Apr-2003	GYM test		2	
102	2-May-2003	Kaliningrad Oblast Championship, Kaliningrad, Russia	1st place	3	
93	22-Nov-2003	Voronezh competition, Russia	8th place	4	
97	23-Apr-2004	Pushkin competition, Russia	1st place	1	**2004 98.4 reps average**
85	2-May-2004	Kaliningrad Oblast Championship, Kaliningrad, Russia (8' on purpose)	1st place	2	
94	22-May-2004	Cup of Russia, Rostov on Don, Russia	7th place	3	
102	9-Oct-2004	Championship of Russia, Gatchina, Russia	8th place	4	
114	20-Nov-2004	Moscow competition, Russia	3rd place	5	
113	6-Mar-2005	Saint Petersburg competition, Russia	1st place	1	**2005 110 reps average**
107	6-Apr-2005	Championship of Russia, Smolensk, Russia	6th place	2	
		Horizontal Bench press 1rep PR - 150kg			**Aug 2005 to Sept 2007**
		Barbell Back Squats 1rep PR - 200kg			
		Barbell Dead Lift 1rep PR - 200kg			
121	28-Jun-2008	International Competition, Novy Svet, Russia	2nd place	1	**2008 110.5 reps average**
100	8-Oct-2008	Pushkin competition, Russia (8' on purpose)	1st place	2	
104	20-Feb-2009	Saint Petersburg competition, Russia	1st place	1	**2009 110.3 reps average**
104	29-Jun-2009	GYM test		2	
124	18-Jul-2009	International Competition, Novy Svet, Russia	2nd place	3	
111	3-Apr-2010	Lipetsk Oblast Championship, Russia (8' on purpose)	1st place	1	**2010 117.5 reps average**
124	13-May-2010	Saint Petersburg competition, Russia	1st place	2	
100	12-Mar-2011	Elec Championship, Russia	1st place	1	**2011**
116	11-Oct-2012	Lipetsk Championship, Russia	2nd place	1	**2012**
		Break from Jerk 2 x 32kg	**2013-2014**		
130	28-Feb-2015	World Championship(WAKSC), Costa Mesa, CA, USA	1st place	1	**2015**
121	27-Feb-2016	World Championship(WAKSC), Costa Mesa, CA, USA	1st place	1	**2016 131.5 reps average**
	13-Aug-2016	Northern California Open Competition, Berkeley, CA, USA	1st place	2	

133	12-Aug-2017	Northern California Open Competition, Berkeley, CA, USA	1st place	1	**2017**
123	1-Dec-2018	Seattle Kettlebell Pro-Am competition, Seattle, WA, USA	1st place	1	**2018 125.5 reps average**
128	8-Dec-2018	Deck to Bells Competition, San Diego, CA, USA	1st place	2	
145	17-Aug-2019	Northern California Open Competition, Berkeley, CA, USA	1st place	1	**2019**
145	25-Feb-2020	GYM test		1	**2020 143.5 reps average**
142	19-Sep-2020	Ballistic Bells Competition, ONLINE	1st place	2	
143	5-Jun-2021	Agatsu Canadian National KB Sport and Mace Championship, ONLINE	1st place	1	**2021**

Fig. 43. Table of 10min Jerk 2x32kg sets (2001-2021)

Snatch Result

My very first attempt for a 10 minute Snatch set with 32kg was on May 9 2002 and I was able to do 72 repetitions (I lasted 5min 20sec). And only on April 6th 2005 I was able to get the full 10 minute of Snatch 32kg with 138 repetitions. Since then, I've completed twenty seven 10 minute sets with 32kg with an average result of 169.1 repetitions. Seven of these were above 200 repetitions, with my highest result of 230 repetitions (130 right arm + 100 left arm) performed in 13 minutes and 11 seconds on January 9, 2014.

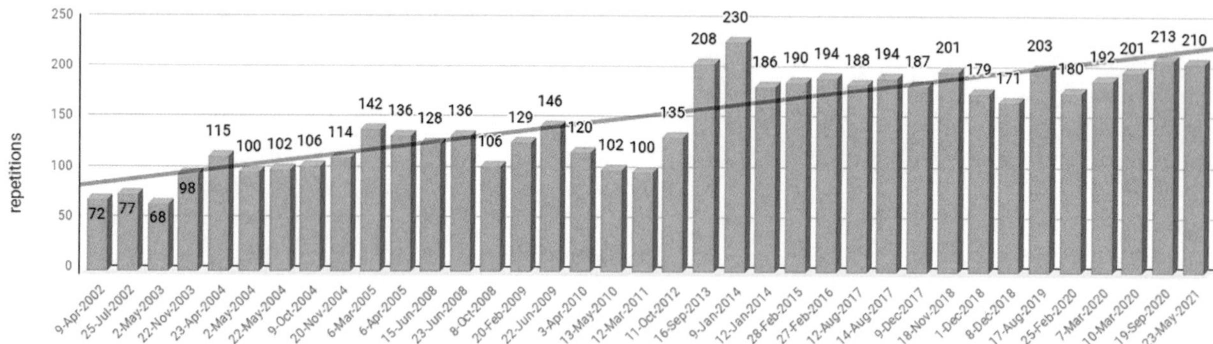

Fig. 44. Chart of 10min Snatch 32kg (2001-2021)

Denis Vasilev Personal Records											
10min Snatch (one-hand switch), reps											
	16kg	**18kg**	**20kg**	**22kg**	**24kg**	**26kg**	**28kg**	**30kg**	**32kg**	**34kg**	**40kg**
second best	255	264	280	240	276	252	240	220	210	126(6')	90(6')
actual	**270**	**276**	**281**	**276**	**281**	**260**	**242**	**222**	**213**	**174(9'35")**	**110(8')**
	27 rpm	27-28 rpm	28 rpm	27-28 rpm	28 rpm	26 rpm	24 rpm	22 rpm	21 rpm	20-18 rpm	15 rpm

Fig. 45. Current snatch records (2021)

Even though I was already performing Snatch since 1999, it took me 14 years before I was finally able to break the 200 repetition barrier in 2013. The key turning point was in 2010 when I was introduced to Sergey Rudnev who accepted me as his student. He coached me in Long Cycle using his then revolutionary training methodology which implemented the use of 2kg increments instead of the traditional 4kg jumps. While Sergey was focused on increasing my personal record in Long Cycle, I used this opportunity to fix my lifting technique.

NOTES	REPS	DATE	EVENT	PLACE	RANK	YEAR
L36+R36 -5min 30sec	72	9-Apr-2002	GYM test		1	**2002 74.5 reps average**
L40+R37 -7min 30sec	77	25-Jul-2002	GYM test		2	
L34+R34 -7min	68	2-May-2003	Kaliningrad Oblast Championship, Kaliningrad, Russia	1st place	1	**2003 83 reps average**
L49+R49 -8min	98	22-Nov-2003	Voronezh competition, Russia	11th place	2	
L55+R60 -8min	115	23-Apr-2004	Pushkin competition, Russia	1st place	1	**2004 107.4 reps average**
L50+R50 80-90% effort	100	2-May-2004	Kaliningrad Oblast Championship, Kaliningrad, Russia	1st place	2	
L51+R51 -7min	102	22-May-2004	Cup of Russia, Rostov on Don, Russia	10th place	3	
L53+R53 -7min	106	9-Oct-2004	Championship of Russia, Gatchina, Russia	9th place	4	
L57+R57 -8min	114	20-Nov-2004	Moscow competition, Russia	8th place	5	
L67+R75 9'30"	142	6-Mar-2005	Saint Petersburg competition, Russia	1st place	1	**2005 139 reps average**
L68+R68	136	6-Apr-2005	Championship of Russia, Smolensk, Russia	6th place	2	
Horizontal Bench press 1rep PR - 150kg						**Aug 2005 to Sept 2007**
Barbell Back Squats 1rep PR - 200kg						
Barbell DeadLift 1rep PR - 200kg						
R64+L64 9min	128	15-Jun-2008	GYM test		1	**2008 123.3 reps average**
R72+L64	136	23-Jun-2008	Kettlebell Clubs competition, Cheboksary, Russia	1st place	2	
R60+L46 7' on purpose	106	8-Oct-2008	Pushkin competition, Russia	1st place	3	
L61+R68	129	20-Feb-2009	Saint Petersburg competition, Russia	1st place	1	**2009 137.5 reps average**
R74+L72	146	22-Jun-2009	Kettlebell Clubs competition, Cheboksary, Russia	1st place	2	
R60+L60 8' on purpose	120	3-Apr-2010	Lipetsk Oblast Championship, Russia	1st place	1	**2010 111 reps average**
R50+L52 7' on purpose	102	13-May-2010	Saint Petersburg competition, Russia	1st place	2	
R50+L50 6' on purpose	100	12-Mar-2011	Elec Championship, Russia	1st place	1	**2011**
R67+L68 9min	135	11-Oct-2012	Lipetsk Championship, Russia	2nd place	1	**2012**
R135+L73 10min 11sec	208	16-Sep-2013	GYM test		1	**2013**

R130+L100 13min 11sec	230	9-Jan-2014	GYM test		1	**2014 208 reps average**
R102+L84	186	12-Jan-2014	EuroFitness GYM Tournament, Russia	1st place	2	
R110+L80	190	28-Feb-2015	World Championship(WAKSC), Costa Mesa, CA, USA	1st place	1	**2015**
R104+L90	194	27-Feb-2016	World Championship(WAKSC), Costa Mesa, CA, USA	1st place	1	**2016**
R94+L94	188	12-Aug-2017	Northern California Open Competition, Berkeley, CA, USA	1st place	1	**2017 189.7 reps average**
R100+L94	194	14-Aug-2017	GYM test		2	
R100+L87	187	9-Dec-2017	Deck to Bells Competition, San Diego, CA, USA	1st place	3	
R110+L91	201	18-Nov-2018	Pendekar Kettlebell Competition, Jakarta, Indonesia	1st place	1	**2018 183.7 reps average**
R94+L85	179	1-Dec-2018	Seattle Kettlebell Pro-Am competition, Seattle, WA, USA	1st place	2	
R80+L91 9min 32sec	171	8-Dec-2018	Deck to Bells Competition, San Diego, CA, USA	1st place	3	
R104+L99	203	17-Aug-2019	Northern California Open Competition, Berkeley, CA, USA	1st place	1	**2019**
R90+L90 9min 30sec	180	25-Feb-2020	GYM test		1	**2020 196.5 reps average**
R105+L87 9min 50sec	192	7-Mar-2020	GYM test		2	
L93+R108 10min 06sec	201	10-Mar-2020	GYM test		3	
R131+L82	213	19-Sep-2020	Ballistic Bells Competition, ONLINE	1st place	4	
R115+L95	210	23-May-2021	North Okanagan Kettlebell Open, ONLINE	1st place	1	**2021**

Fig. 46. Table of 10min Snatch 32kg sets (2001-2021)

Later in 2012, I adapted the use of 2kg increments for my Snatch training and the result was just mind blowing. I elevated my Snatch numbers from a paltry 142 repetitions to a phenomenal 208 repetitions (a 146% increase!) on September 16 2013. Despite the fact that I achieved this result in the gym, my result matched the current world record in my weight class! Since then, I have performed consistently well in Snatch and so far my best competition result was on September 19 2020 with 213 repetitions.*

* Ballistic Bells Online Competition (September 19 2020 - California, USA): https://youtu.be/WP8up3vqleo

Biathlon Result

I participated in my very first 10 minute Biathlon competition with 32kg on May 2 2003 and immediately achieved the rank of Master of Sport with 136 points*. Since then, I've done twenty three Biathlon competitions with 32kg and my average score is 183.6 points. Eight of these were above the requirements for MSIC and my best result so far was on September 19 2020 with 248.5 points.

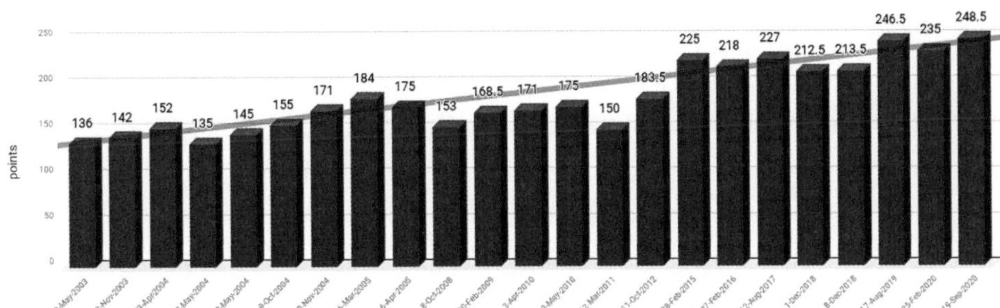

Fig. 47. Chart of 10min Biathlon 32kg (2001-2021)

BIATHLON points = Jerk reps + 1/2 Snatch reps

Fig. 48. Biathlon score calculation

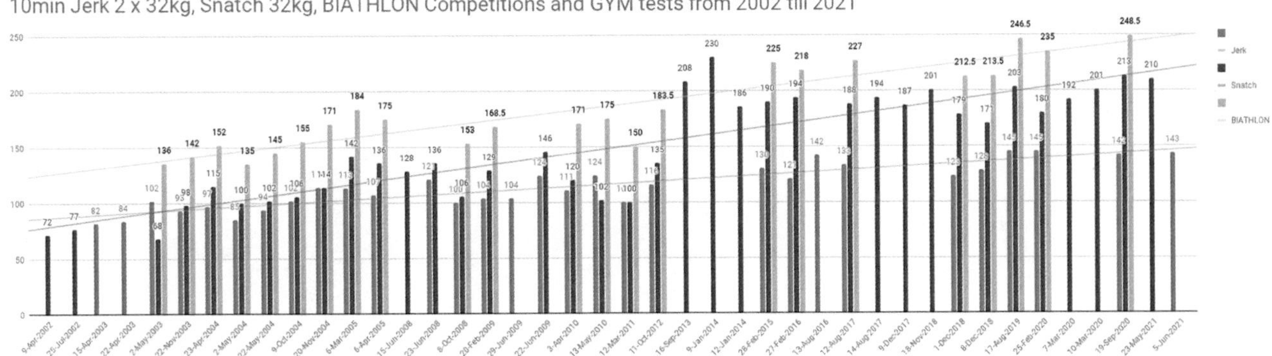

Fig. 49. Bar graph results of 10min Biathlon 32kg (2001-2021)

* The score for Biathlon is the number of Jerk repetitions plus half the number of Snatch repetitions. For example, 100 repetitions in Jerk and 200 repetitions in Snatch equals 200 points total.

I haven't counted all the other 10 minute Biathlon sets I've done with lighter weights, but below is a chart showing my top two best results for every kettlebell weight I've ever used.

Denis Vasilev Personal Records									
10min BIATHLON, reps									
	16kg	**18kg**	**20kg**	**22kg**	**24kg**	**26kg**	**28kg**	**30kg**	**32kg**
second best			368		340		273.5	247	246.5
actual	**385**	**368**	**369**	**370**	**343**	**311**	**278**	**274**	**248.5**

Fig. 50. Current biathlon records (2021)

Even though I was able to immediately become a Master of Sport in Biathlon, I've always felt that I was more of a strength athlete rather than an endurance athlete. Long Cycle has always been more enjoyable to me but it may be that it was not until recently that my technique improvements finally allowed me to enjoy Biathlon. Indeed, after my lifting technique issues were solved I started to grow fond of Biathlon and wanted to increase my results to MSIC standards. I finally achieved this goal on February 28 2015 when I got 225 points, 8 points more than the required score for MSIC. I eventually surpassed this on September 19 2020 when I got my current record of 248.5 points.

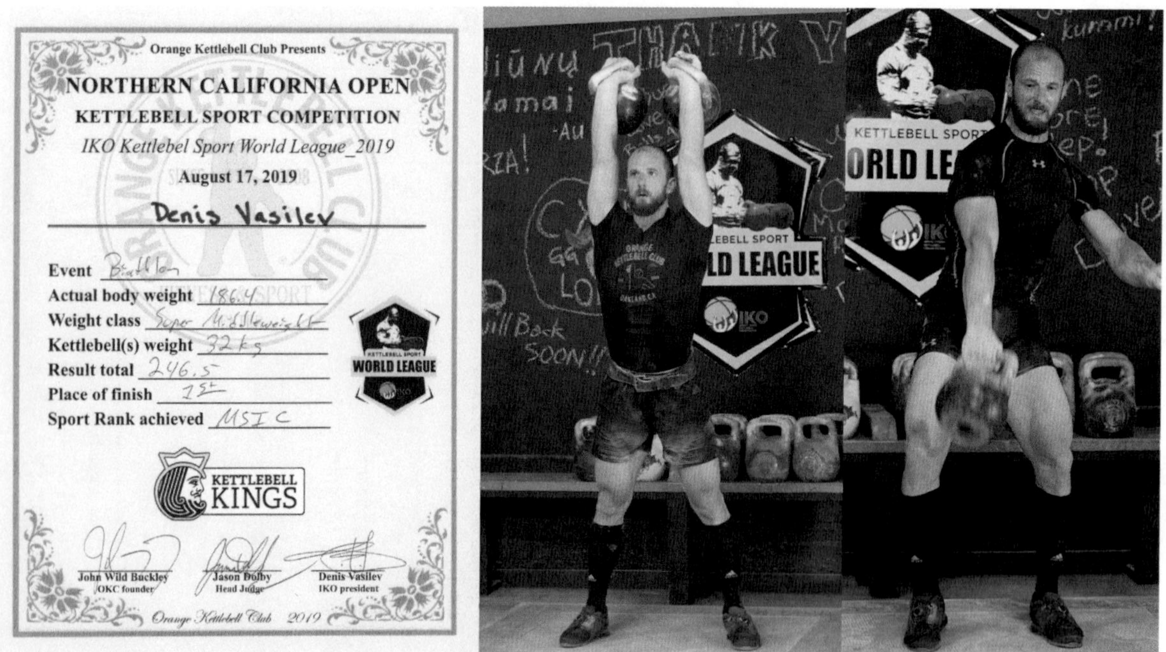
Orange Kettlebell Club Presents
NORTHERN CALIFORNIA OPEN
KETTLEBELL SPORT COMPETITION
IKO Kettlebel Sport World League_2019
August 17, 2019
Denis Vasilev
Event Biathlon
Actual body weight 186.4
Weight class Super Middleweight
Kettlebell(s) weight 32 kg
Result total 246.5
Place of finish 1st
Sport Rank achieved MSIC
KETTLEBELL KINGS
John Wild Buckley, OKC founder
Jason Dolby, Head Judge
Denis Vasilev, IKO president
Orange Kettlebell Club 2019

NorCal 2019 Competition Diploma; Jerk and Snatch performance

POINTS	DATE	EVENT	PLACE	RANK		YEAR
136 (J 102, Sn 68)	2-May-2003	Kaliningrad Oblast Championship, Kaliningrad, Russia	1st place	**MS**	1	**2003 139 points average**
142 (J 93, Sn 98)	22-Nov-2003	Voronezh competition, Russia	8th place	MS	2	
154.5 (J 97, Sn 115)	23-Apr-2004	Pushkin competition, Russia	1st place	**MS**	1	**2004 151.6 reps average**
135 (J 85, Sn 100)	2-May-2004	Kaliningrad Oblast Championship, Kaliningrad, Russia	1st place	**MS**	2	
145 (J 94, Sn 102)	22-May-2004	Cup of Russia, Rostov on Don, Russia	6th place	**MS**	3	
155 (J 102, Sn 106)	9-Oct-2004	Championship of Russia, Gatchina, Russia	9th place	**MS**	4	
171 (J 114, Sn 114)	20-Nov-2004	Moscow competition, Russia	8th place	**MS**	5	
184 (J 113, Sn 142)	6-Mar-2005	Saint Petersburg competition, Russia	1st place	**MS**	1	**2005 179.5 points average**
175 (J 107, Sn 136)	6-Apr-2005	Championship of Russia, Smolensk, Russia	6th place	**MS**	2	
Horizontal Bench press 1rep PR - 150kg						**Aug 2005 to Sept 2007**
Barbell Back Squats 1rep PR - 200kg						
Barbell DeadLift 1rep PR - 200kg						
153 (J 100, Sn 106)	8-Oct-2008	Pushkin Town competition, Russia (8'Jerk, 7' Snatch on purpose)	1st place	**MS**	1	**2008**
168.5 (J 104, Sn 129)	20-Feb-2009	Saint Petersburg competition, Russia	1st place	**MS**	1	**2009**
171 (J 111, Sn 120)	3-Apr-2010	Lipetsk Oblast Championship, Russia (8'Jerk, 8' Snatch on purpose)	1st place	**MS**	1	**2010 173 points average**
175 (J 124, Sn 102)	13-May-2010	Saint Petersburg competition, Russia (7' Snatch on purpose)	1st place	**MS**	2	
150 (J 100, Sn 100)	12-Mar-2011	Elec Championship, Russia (6' Snatch on purpose)	1st place	**MS**	1	**2011**
183.5 (J 116, Sn 135)	11-Oct-2012	Lipetsk Championship, Russia	2nd place	**MS**	1	**2012**
Break from BIATHLON 2 x 32kg				**2013 - 2014**		
225 (J 130, Sn 190)	28-Feb-2015	World Championship(WAKSC), Costa Mesa, CA, USA	1st place	**MSIC**	1	**2015**

218 (J 121, Sn 194)	27-Feb-2016	World Championship(WAKSC), Costa Mesa, CA, USA	1st place	**MSIC**	1	**2016**
227 (J 133, Sn 188)	12-Aug-2017	Northern California Open Competition, Berkeley, CA, USA	1st place	**MSIC**	1	**2017**
212.5 (J 123, Sn 179)	1-Dec-2018	Seattle Kettlebell Pro-Am competition, Seattle, WA, USA	1st place	MSIC	1	**2018** **213 points average**
213.5 (J 128, Sn 171)	8-Dec-2018	Deck to Bells Competition, San Diego, CA, USA	1st place	**MSIC**	2	
246.5 (J 145, Sn 203)	17-Aug-2019	Northern California Open Competition, Berkeley, CA, USA	1st place	**MSIC**	1	**2019**
235 (J 145, Sn 180)	25-Feb-2020	GYM test		**MSIC**	1	**2020**
248.5 (J 142, Sn 213)	19-Sep-2020	Ballistic Bells Competition, ONLINE	1st place	**MSIC**	1	**2021**

Fig. 51. Table of 10min Biathlon 32kg sets (2001-2021)

PART 3
Final Words

A training program has many moving parts that need to be organized in a systematic and logical way. From selecting the types of workouts, to determining the amount of sets and exercises with the appropriate rest periods, to choosing the correct kettlebell weights, you have at your disposal nearly an overwhelmingly infinite set of possible combinations. This is why I recommend that every athlete and coach first experiment on themselves before implementing their training program on another person. The best way to carry out the experiment would be to have an experienced coach guide you from start to finish. It usually takes about 3 cycles of 10-12 weeks each (about 9 months in total) before you can honestly say that you have gained a deep feel and understanding for the program. The best confirmation that your chosen method was successful is when you are able to achieve the rank of Candidate Master Of Sport or higher with it. Only then can you recommend your program to others.

With regard to training and programming there are principal rules that are essential and universal. However, improvisation is a big part of the training process. A successful coach is not only familiar with their training method, but they also have the ability to "hear and feel" their students and are able to use that feedback to customize the training plan.

When you are uncertain about what kind of workout to perform next, you should always lean towards doing a moderate and less challenging session. Safe always works. If the workout turns out to be easy, you can make it more challenging by reducing the rest periods or by increasing the lifting pace. This will provide a positive mental benefit for the athlete because they will feel that the workout was completed with less effort than expected. I cannot understate the importance of the emotional satisfaction experienced by the athlete after such a workout.

On the other hand, if the workout turns out to be above the athlete's current abilities, you can make it easier by either extending the rest between sets or by decreasing the lifting pace. Besides risking injuries and overtraining, the negative mental harm on the athlete must be avoided as much as possible. Frustration and depression caused by being unable to comply with the plan can hurt an athlete's motivation to continue training.

Coaches, respect and love your athletes. They entrust their lives to you and you must care for them as you would your own life. No matter how high our ambitions are, we must not forget that health and safety are the most important priorities in an athlete's career. Should you find yourself in a position where victory lies at the cost of the athlete's health, you need to choose health. This way they will have a chance for another shot at victory.

Thank you for reading my book and I hope this will help you achieve the utmost success in your kettlebell sport training.

https://orangekettlebellclub.com

After workout at the Orange Kettlebell Club

Bibliography

1. Vasilev D.U. Metodika trenirovki visokokvalifitsirovannikh girevokov [Elite kettlebell lifters training methodology]: Degree work. – The Lesgaft National State University of Physical Education, Sport and Health, St.-Petersburg, 2015. – 61 p.
2. Vinogradov, G.P. Atletizm: teoria I metodika trenirovki [Athleticism: Training theory and practice]: textbook for academies – M.: Soviet sport, 2009. – 328 p.: ill.
3. Vorotintsev, A.I. Giri – sport silnikh I zdorovikh [Kettlebell sport for strength and health]. – M.: Soviet sport. 2002. – 270 p.
4. Gorbov, A.M. Girevoy sport [Kettlebell sport]/auth. – co-auth. A.M. Gorbov. – M.: AST; G51 Donetsk: Stalker, 2006. – 191 p.: ill.
5. Zaitsev Y.M., Ivanov Y.I., Petrov V.K. Zanimaites girevim sportom [Practice kettlebell lifting]. – M.: Soviet sport, 1991 – 48 p., ill.
6. Iliin, E.P. Motivatsiya I motive [Motivation] / E.P. Iliin. – SPb.: Piter. 2000. – 512 p.: ill.
7. Kots, Y.M. Fiziologiya mishechnoy deyatelnosti [Physiology of muscle activity]: textbook for physical culture academies. / Y.M. Kots – red. – M.: PiS, 1982. – 340 p.
8. Kuramshin, Y.F. Teoriya I metodika fizicheskoy kultury [Theory and methodology of physical culture] / Y.P. Kuramshin. – M.: 2007. – 441 p.
9. Kuramshin, Y.F. Podgotovka sportsmena v processe trenirovki [Athele's preparation in training process]// V kN. Theory and practice of physical culture: Textbook./ Y.F. Kuramshin, O.A. Dveirina, V.P. Aksenov, / Under prof. Kuramshin red. – M.: Soviet sport, 2003 – 356-389 p.
10. Muminov, V.I. Gireviy sport [Kettlebell sport]: Tutorial. – St. Petersburg, Military University of Physical Culture, 1995. – 108p.
11. Nosov, G.V. Girevoy sport [Kettlebell sport]: Tutorial. / G.V. Nosov; Smolensk State Universily of Physical Culture. – Smolensk, 1998. – 56 p.
12. Odintsov, A.G. Girevoye dvoeborije [Kettlebell Biathlon]: Tutoria. – M.: Academy of Economic Safety MIA of Russian Federation, 2004. – 48 p.
13. Samsonova, A.V. Biomekhanika mishts [Muscle biomechanics]: Teaching aid / A.V. Samsonova, E.N. Komissarova / under A.V. Samsonova red. / The Lesgaft National State University of Physical Education, Sport and Health, St.-Petersburg.: [b.n.], 2008. – 127 p.
14. Seroklistov, I.I. Girevoy sport. Pedagogicheskiye osnovy trenirovki girevikov [Kettlebell sport. Pedagogical basis of kettlebell lifters' training]/ I.I. Seroklistov; Moscow Timiryazev Agriculture Academy. – M., 1996. – 32 p.
15. Solodkov, A.S. Fiziologiya cheloveka [Human Physiology]. / A.S. Solodkov, E.B. Sologub – M.: Terra-Sport, 2001. – 540 p.
16. Tikhonov, V.F. Osnovy girevogo sporta: obucheniye dvigatelnym deystviyam I metody trenirovki [Basis of kettlebell sport: teaching motor actions and training methods]: tutorial. – M.: Soviet sport, 2009. – 132 p.

Bibliography

Made in the USA
Las Vegas, NV
10 December 2023